P9-EDH-685

LIBERATED
Quiltmaking II
GWEN MARSTON

American Quilter's Society
P. O. Box 3290 • Paducah, KY 42002-3290
www.AmericanQuilter.com

Located in Paducah, Kentucky, the American Quilter's Society (AQS) is dedicated to promoting the accomplishments of today's quilters. Through its publications and events, AQS strives to honor today's quiltmakers and their work and to inspire future creativity and innovation in quiltmaking.

EXECUTIVE BOOK EDITOR: ANDI MILAM REYNOLDS
BOOK EDITOR: DARRA WILLIAMSON
GRAPHIC DESIGN: ELAINE WILSON
COVER DESIGN: MICHAEL BUCKINGHAM
PHOTOGRAPHY: CHARLES R. LYNCH, FINISHED PROJECTS UNLESS OTHERWISE NOTED

All rights reserved. No part of this book may be reproduced, stored in any retrieval system, or transmitted in any form, or by any means including but not limited to electronic, mechanical, photocopy, recording, or otherwise, without the written consent of the author and publisher. Patterns may be copied for personal use only. While every effort has been made to ensure that the contents of this publication are as accurate and correct as possible, no warranty is provided nor results guaranteed. Since the author and AQS have no control over individual skills or choice of materials and tools, they do not assume responsibility for the use of this information.

Additional copies of this book may be ordered from the American Quilter's Society, PO Box 3290, Paducah, KY 42002-3290, or online at www.AmericanQuilter.com.

Text © 2010, Author, Gwen Marston
Artwork © 2010, American Quilter's Society

Library of Congress Cataloging-in-Publication Data

Marston, Gwen

Liberated Quiltmaking/Gwen Marston.

p. cm.

ISBN 0-89145-878-6

1. Patchwork. 2. Patchwork – Patterns. 3. Quilting. 4. Quilting – Patterns. 5. Patchwork quilts. I. Title.

TT835.M2724   1996   96-36321

746.46-dc20   CIP

American Quilter's Society
P. O. Box 3290 • Paducah, KY 42002-3290
www.AmericanQuilter.com

DEDICATION

Since 1990 I have had the pleasure of teaching Liberated Quiltmaking classes all over the United States, and in Japan, New Zealand, and England. This book is dedicated to all the quilters whom I've met in these classes. Meeting these quilters—with their open minds and their interest in exploring new ideas—has given me a great deal of pleasure. I also take this opportunity to thank them for coming to my classes, for if they hadn't, I wouldn't have been there either. It has been a wonderful experience for me, and I sincerely thank you, one and all.

LEFT: CABBAGES AND ROSES, detail. Full quilt on page 92.

TITLE PAGE: SAWTOOTH IN BARS, 41" x 44", 2009. Made and hand quilted by the author.

Table of CONTENTS

LEFT AND OPPOSITE: SAMPLER WITH STRING BLOCKS AND APPLIQUÉ BORDER, detail. Full quilt shown on page 113.

LIBERATED QUILTMAKING: Quilts Without Restrictions

Discovering quilts was a life-changing event for me. I went to an exhibit of antique quilts at my local art museum and it was as though I had "a calling," which I gladly accepted with enthusiasm and determination. I couldn't get enough, and I began studying old quilts for ideas and then tried to make them.

Initially, with very few exceptions, I liked every quilt I saw, but eventually I realized that the quilts that really tantalized me were the unorthodox quilts—the ones that held surprises. These quilts didn't have obvious explanations. They didn't appear to be made from commercial patterns, nor did they pay any attention whatsoever to the contemporary "rules and regulations" set forth by the quilt "authorities" of the day. The CRAZY COTTON QUILT TOP shown on page 7 is an example of the free-spirited quilts that I found intriguing. Because there is more to see and more to figure out, quilts like this hold my attention longer than their predictable, well-organized, color-coordinated, pattern-based, uptown sisters.

It wasn't long before I began experimenting with sewing leftover scraps together into small, freeform compositions in an attempt to mirror what I was seeing. I think my first finished quilt in this style was a little freeform Log Cabin quilt that I made in 1987. A few years later, I sewed a stray triangle to one of these little experiments, and—lo and behold—it looked rather like a house. This was the moment of discovery; it was as though I'd opened a door, walked into a very large, empty room as the lights and the music came up, and I found myself in a whole new world of infinite possibilities.

Realizing that I could make House blocks without a pattern meant that there were likely many other blocks I could make using this new freeform, free-pieced, innovative, and improvisational process. While those are all words that describe this way of working, I eventually settled on the phrase "Liberated Quiltmaking" because that was the way it made me feel. *Liberated Quiltmaking* (American Quilter's Society, 1996) also became the title of my first book on the subject. Now here we are, 14 years later, continuing our exploration in this sequel.

By the time *Liberated Quiltmaking* was published, I'd come to understand that certain groups of people were particularly comfortable with making wildly innovative quilts. It was clear that African-American quilters had a special ability to make bold, innovative and—dare I say it—"liberated" quilts. At the time, African-American quilters had begun to attract attention and, with the unveiling of the Gee's Bend quilts in 2002, most quilters now understand the important contribution these inventive women made. The Bibliography (page 125) gives a listing of books that feature African-American quilts.

Another group who managed to make lively,

original, artistic quilts—regardless of race—were rural people. Many of these fearless quilters were from the South. Some of these women were poor, so they used what they had, which wasn't very much. One kind of quilt that lent itself well to taming unruly scraps was the string quilt, made by piecing scraps to a foundation. I have always loved the idea that people of few means made some of the most original and artistic quilts. I think of these quilts as the Jackson Pollocks of the quilt world.

My excitement about exploring new Liberated ways of making quilts has not diminished since I first discovered it. This second volume includes several updated lessons and seven quilts from the first book. The remainder of the book introduces new Liberated ideas, and quilts developed and made in the ensuing years. One of the best things about Liberated Quiltmaking is that it provides a way for you to make original work. In fact you will be making quilts so original that you won't be able to copy yourself. I invite you to join me in the exploration of Liberated Quiltmaking, of making quilts without restrictions.

CRAZY COTTON QUILT TOP, maker unknown, c. 1920–1940

The NON-RULES of Design

Liberated Quiltmaking offers a process rather than a pattern. Process gives you a way of working, a way to make quilts that are uniquely your own. This book is not project-oriented; instead, it shows new ways to make the components used in a quilt and leaves details—such as how big your quilt will be—up to you.

I've always thought making quilts was like cooking, and I've guessed that people make quilts the way they cook. Some get out the recipe and follow it exactly. Others refer to recipes from time to time to refresh their memories about spices or ingredients, but usually they just start cooking, tasting periodically and adding what's needed. I'm this second kind of a cook, and that's the way I make my quilts too. Here's how it works:

- I understand the basic concepts involved in cooking.
- I have a pretty good idea about what the main ingredients are.
- I start cooking and season to taste as I go along.

Finding Inspiration

If you start looking carefully at the details in antique quilts, you will find that our quilting ancestors were a lot more Liberated than they have been given credit for. As I mentioned on page 6, I admire African-American quilts and string quilts for their Liberated spirit. The Bibliography (page 125) lists books in my library with photos that have inspired me and might well inspire you.

Since you have this book, why not look here for some inspiration? Study the quilts for basic ideas and details that speak to you, and that you might use in your work. The great thing about Liberated Quiltmaking is that you are working with a process, not a pattern, so you get to interpret ideas rather than copy someone else's design.

Getting Started

As with most things in life, the hardest part is getting started. You need a general idea, and the rest will come to you when you need it—it really will. I see it in my classes all the time.

Designing as You Go

Start with a little idea and see where it takes you. You don't need to have the entire quilt figured out before you begin. In fact, if you plan it as you sew it, your planning time lasts until the quilt is done, so you actually spend more time planning than if you tried to plan before you started sewing. Therefore, *don't* choose all the colors, *don't* precut the entire quilt, *don't* worry about running out of fabric, *don't* worry about what size the quilt is going to be or how you are going to quilt it; that will all come to you in good time. To summarize: Don't commit too soon. These are words to live by.

> Don't precut fabric for the entire quilt before you begin. Cut the pieces for one block and see how it goes together. Make a few blocks and play around with them. You may decide to change the size of some units by making them a bit smaller or a bit larger.

Choosing Colors

It all works. You don't need to reinvent the wheel. With such a rich tradition of quilting, there are many quilts to study for color possibilities. Look carefully at the quilts you are drawn to and analyze the color schemes. Here is a review of the points I made about color in my first book about Liberated Quiltmaking.

- You don't need to choose all the colors before you start sewing.
- Consider adding accent colors.
- Trust yourself when choosing colors.
- It's harder to make a mistake than you think.
- It's easier to err by playing it too safe: over-coordination can lead to the "color by number" look and a monotonous quilt.
- The more fabrics you use in a quilt, the less important each specific fabric becomes.
- Sometimes one color will help unify a quilt.
- Study other quilts for color ideas.

Figuring Out the Piecing

When you're trying to figure out how to go about making a new Liberated block or quilt, make a rough sketch of what you'd like to make. That will help you see how to go about piecing it. If you still aren't certain, sketch the block full size. This gives you an even clearer idea of how to make your plan work. You can check the scale of the design and get an idea about how big to cut the pieces. These drawings then work like your map. They are your guides as you begin your work. For example, when you've learned the basics of building a simple Liberated Basket, you can move on to making much more complex blocks. A sketch will help you figure out how to construct it. You will be able to see what parts need to be made first to avoid complicated set-in seams.

Running Out of Fabric

This is a part of quiltmaking, so you might as well get over stewing about it right now. I know how quilters deal with running out of fabric because I spend a lot of time with quilters. Here is the common scenario. When you run out, you jump in your car and drive to the quilt shop. If the fabric you want isn't there, you drive around to all the other quilt shops in the area. Then you go home and call your friends whom you most suspect have some of "your" fabric. After that you go on the Internet.

I have a great solution for this problem. When you run out of fabric, substitute another fabric. Listen, this is how it has been done for a couple of hundred years. In fact, this is why antique quilts often have an edge over contemporary quilts. In looking at antique quilts, you see that sometimes quilters substituted a color and print that was close to what they had been using. Sometimes it was the same color, but a different tone, and

sometimes it was completely different. The result of fabric substitution was so often a quilt with depth and an element of surprise. It can be this kind of unpredictable touch that makes a quilt artful. Remember, the great painters we hold in high esteem weren't those whose chosen medium was paint by number.

Quiltmaking as Play

Don't stress out. It won't help a bit. Most of us aren't quilting to add more stress to our lives. Contrary to popular belief, you don't have to suffer to make a good quilt. Chances are, if you see this as "play time at the sewing machine," your work will reflect your good mood. Most of us do better work if we're doing it with a positive attitude and a happy heart. Maybe that wasn't true for Van Gogh, but still, most people are more successful when they're feeling confident and excited about the adventure they have embarked upon.

I think your chances for doing something innovative, something beyond what you think your capabilities are, improve when you plunge ahead. Just start making something. Make something small. Write your own rules, and don't try to be "arty." (That won't help.) I'm not kidding about this. Life is short. Do your own work, have a good time, and be nice to everybody...including yourself.

LEFT: LIBERATED LOG CABIN WITH STRING BORDER, detail. Full quilt on page 18.

The INS and OUTS of Liberated Construction

One of my favorite country blues songs by the great Big Bill Broonzy acknowledges, "When things go wrong, so wrong with you, it hurts me too." As a quilt teacher, when things go wrong with you, it really does hurt me too, because I feel I haven't done my job satisfactorily. When I'm teaching, and students have problems, it means I need to review my lesson plans, and I do. So here's a dose of old-fashioned wisdom about such matters: There is always a way to fix something.

Problem Solving

We all know the phrase "the mother of invention." Well, quilters, that's us! We can solve our own problems. Our quilting ancestors living out on the farm had to solve their own problems, and—because they were sensible and practical people—they solved them in the most sensible, practical ways. One of the things I like best about antique quilts is discovering the ways quilters worked out their technical and design problems, and how these unpredictable choices added appreciably to the artistic interest and success of the work. It's the unpredictability that creates intrigue.

My advice is to stop thinking about the "right" way to fix something and start thinking about the "smart" way, the practical way to make it work.

There is more than one way of doing most things that need to be done. This isn't rocket science; all we are doing is sewing pieces of fabric together.

Figure It Out as You Go

As you work, you'll naturally refine your techniques and find easier methods for accomplishing your goals. Liberated Quiltmaking is all experimental work, so you get to stay engaged all the way through the process. I find myself constantly wondering about other ways, better ways of doing things. It's helpful for the Liberated Quiltmaker to be adventuresome, willing to make mistakes, and to thrive on figuring out ways to make things work. It also helps to be a quiltmaker who enjoys the experience for the "whole ride."

A Word About the Rotary Cutter

Using a phrase from my parents' generation, I'd like to start by saying, "For crying out loud," keep a sharp blade in your rotary cutter! We all make the mistake of thinking we can use the blade just a little bit longer. Then when we eventually do change the blade, we are shocked—just shocked!—at how much easier our work becomes. So do yourself a favor: Keep a sharp blade in the cutter and don't forget to close it the moment you put it down. (These are both very good habits to develop.)

Pressing

I press a lot as I build the units and sew them together. Pressing helps me keep things flat, and shows me when I need to straighten an edge. Pressing (and keeping the edges of the units and or blocks straight) ensures that your finished quilt will lie flat. I often remind quilters that working in the Liberated style doesn't mean you have to throw the baby out with the bathwater.

Ripping Out

Rarely does a quilt get made without some ripping involved. In Liberated Quiltmaking, however, ripping sometimes can be replaced simply by cutting off the "mistake" at the offending seam. So, before you automatically rip something apart, consider whether a little creative cutting and resewing might work just as well. With Liberated block construction, who would know one way or the other?

In Conclusion...

...get ready to have some fun! The great thing about Liberated construction methods is that they provide an accessible path to original work. In fact, you'll be so original, you won't be able to copy yourself! It's a wonderfully entertaining way to work, and it's never boring. Each block you make is a different composition, and you get to make all the decisions, so you are constantly thinking about what you might try next.

You can—and you should—find your own comfort level in terms of the way you like to sew and the type of quilt you prefer. You can take this as far as you like: You can put your toe in, or jump right off the deep end.

Although I provide step-by-step instruction for each process in this book, remember this: In the world of Liberated Quiltmaking, there are endless options. Feel free to make any changes that wander across your imagination.

And lastly, remember the golden rule of Liberated Quiltmaking:

If something is too big, cut it off;
if something is too small, add on.

LEFT: CRAZY COTTON QUILT TOP, detail. Full quilt on page 7.

PROCESS

1: Liberated Log Cabins

Giving credit where credit is due, my ideas for this type of work came directly from antique quilts and blocks such as the ones shown on this page. I made my first Liberated Log Cabin quilt in 1987, and of all the Liberated ideas I've explored since, I have returned most often to Log Cabins. This block seems to hold myriad artistic possibilities. It can be simple or complex. It can include many angles or few angles. It can be made with large or small pieces. It can be made in a wide or a limited number of fabrics and colors. The six quilts shown in this chapter were chosen to demonstrate the wide variation of artistic ideas this block brings to the table.

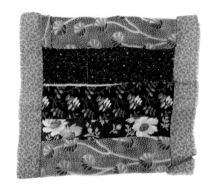

Having made quite a few Liberated Log Cabin quilts, I've discovered that it works well to begin by laying out some basic guidelines. Let's look at the quilts shown in this chapter, and I'll explain what my "recipe" was for each one.

Antique blocks, 1880. Collection of the author. Blocks like these old beauties inspired me to get "Liberated" more than 100 years later.

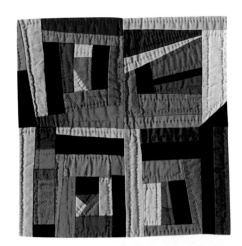

Let's Look at the Quilts

LIBERATED LOG CABIN WITH BROWN BORDER was an effort to make a quilt that used artistic ideas commonly seen in Amish quilts of a similar style made in the early 1900s. Characteristics of these quilts include blocks made of odd-shaped scraps in solid colors; cotton crazy-quilt-like construction; wide borders pieced from fabrics in different tones of the same color; quilted cables that run off the ends instead of turning the corners; and 1" wide finished binding cut on the straight of the goods.

LIBERATED LOG CABIN WITH BROWN BORDER, 42" x 49", 2000.
Made and hand quilted by the author.

When I made MY MOOSE QUILT, the guiding principle was to make an outdoorsy-looking quilt, reminiscent of a mackinaw jacket. I was going for a flat, understated look, and I thought the moose would appreciate the low contrast. (Typically, moose prefer to blend in and not be noticed.) The blocks begin with centers of slightly different sizes, cut specifically to feature a moose in each one. From there, I built the blocks outward with strips of different widths, and then squared the blocks to the same size before sewing them into rows. The name of the quilt, my name, the date, pine trees, leaves, a moon, and several moose lurk in the borders.

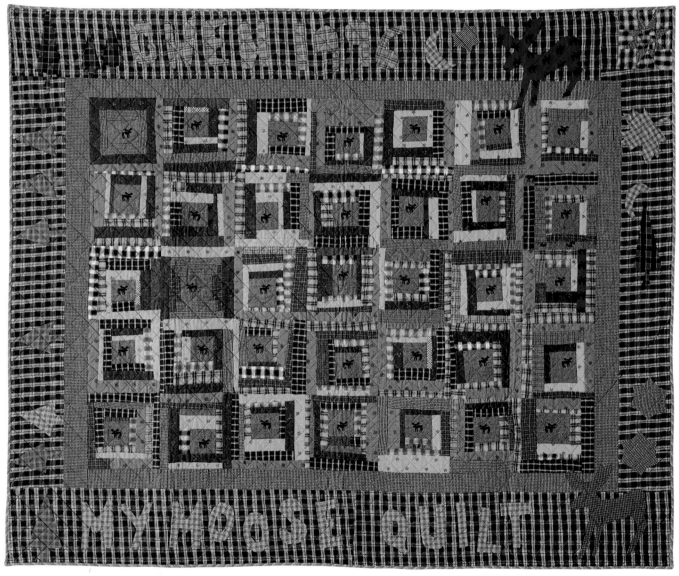

MY MOOSE QUILT, 56" x 69", 1996. Made and machine quilted by the author.

LIBERATED LOG CABIN FOR AMBER, 64" x 72", 2005. Made by author and machine quilted by Robyn House. Collection of Amber Joy.

I made LIBERATED LOG CABIN FOR AMBER (page 16) for my sister, and I wanted something splashy and wildly cheerful for her, which dictated the fabric choices. I also decided I'd started each block with a four-patch arrangement that featured a lively fabric with large dots.

In LIBERATED LOG CABIN WITH STRING BORDER (page 18), the blocks were sewn together in clumps and rows. The way to figure out how it was assembled is by following the seam lines. This is perhaps the most abstract of the quilts in this chapter. It was made from "found scraps" I gathered at my 2008 Beaver Island Quilt Retreat. By found scraps, I literally mean scraps the other quilters had discarded—sometimes on the floor. Actually, using little, odd-shaped "leftovers" is the easiest way to make an abstract quilt with a real scrappy flavor. That's because you're working with the odd shapes you're given; it's simply a matter of accepting the gift and sewing the pieces together any way you can manage it. The design work is pretty much eliminated, and it would be hard to be as inventive if you began with a pile of uncut, coordinated fabrics.

LIBERATED LOG CABIN MEDALLION (page 19) takes the basic concept of this block to another level. Here the Log Cabin is celebrated as one large, uncomplicated block. Using quilting ideas I borrowed from our quilting sisters in India and Pakistan, I used close, straight lines of quilting to fill the large, open spaces, which created wonderful texture.

LIBERATED LOG CABIN (page 20) is another in my series of quilts exploring the idea of the quilt as one simple, abstract Liberated Log Cabin block. I hand quilted this quilt in what I think of as my "tribal quilting" style: close, straight-line stitching and other, unmarked freeform shapes. The idea is to figure out what to quilt as the work is in progress. Since I hand quilt in a frame, I have lots of time to think about what to quilt, and therefore I think I make better choices. Notice how thoughtful quilting can enhance even the most simple of quilts and how the stitching shows up especially well on solid fabrics.

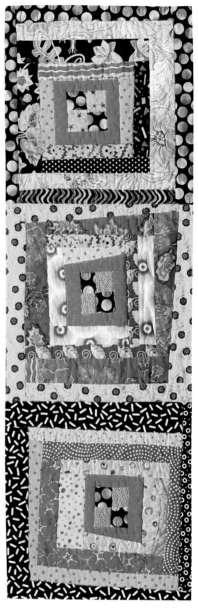

LIBERATED LOG CABIN FOR AMBER, detail

Here's a little tip I've discovered by making lots of quilts: The best way to make a scrap quilt that looks authentic is to make it from *scraps*.

LIBERATED LOG CABIN WITH STRING BORDER, 34" x 35", 2009. Made and hand quilted by the author.

LIBERATED LOG CABIN MEDALLION, 41" x 44", 2009. Made and hand
quilted by the author.

LIBERATED LOG CABIN, 37" x 37", 2009. Made and hand quilted by the author. Fabrics hand dyed by Kathy Swanteck.

Liberated Log Cabin Fundamentals

Traditional Log Cabin blocks are made with strips of equal width sewn in specific arrangements of lights and darks in a predetermined configuration. Not so with Liberated Log Cabin blocks.

Here is an expanded overview of Liberated Log Cabin fundamentals.

- As you work, think of each block as a single composition.
- The center need not be a square—although it can be a "squarish" shape—and can be the same size or vary from block to block. You can also begin with something other than a square, such as a half-square triangle, a four-patch unit, or some other shape. The center can be large or small in proportion to the finished block.
- The strips can be fairly close to the same width...or not.
- The order in which you add the strips doesn't matter.
- The color arrangement doesn't matter.
- Blocks can be squared to the same size, or sized the same in one dimension only. When sized the same in one dimension only, the blocks in one row won't line up with the blocks in adjacent rows, as you clearly can see in the LIBERATED LOG CABIN WITH STRING BORDER (page 18), detail. This is okay!

> ### Basic Concept
> Cut a square or "squarish" shape, build around it with oddly sized and shaped pieces, and then square the block to size in one or both directions.

LIBERATED LOG CABIN WITH STRING BORDER, detail. Full quilt on page 18. When blocks are sized the same in one dimension only, the blocks in one row won't line up with those in adjacent rows, making for an even more Liberated Quilt.

Fig. 1

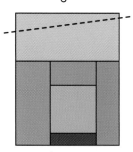

Fig. 2

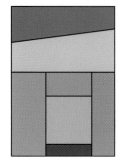

Fig. 3

Step-by-Step: Liberated Log Cabin Block

1. Cut a square or "squarish" shape by eye (fig. 1).

2. Cut some strips of different widths, and add them to the center in any order. Press and straighten the edges as you work. Don't cut all the strips at once. Get started and then make your choices.

3. Angles are easy to add by sewing on a straight piece and then cutting the straight edge at an angle (fig. 2). Add another straight piece, press, and straighten the edge (fig. 3).

4. Make a bunch of blocks, building them up until they are all about the same size, and trim them to the desired measurements. Remember: You have the option of making them square, or trimming them to the same height or width so that you can sew them into rows. If you choose the second option, you'll need either to add on or trim off a few blocks to make the rows come out even.

What If...

...you add "slivers" of an accent color to some of your blocks? That's an idea I've used to good effect. A see-through quilter's ruler is helpful because you can follow the ¼" marking line and adjust the ruler to create a slim angled piece (fig. 4). If you are working with prints, try using a solid as an accent. If working with solids, choose a print as an accent.

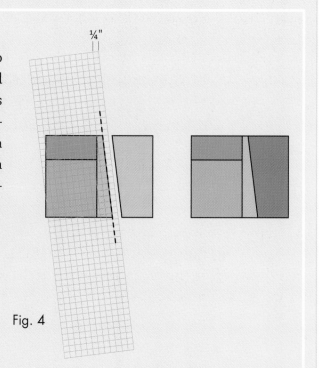

Fig. 4

P R O C E S S 2: Base-Block Construction

The Star block provided one of my first explorations into the world of Liberated Quiltmaking, and my first Liberated Star quilt was shown at The National Quilt Museum of the United States (formerly the Museum of the American Quilter's Society, or MAQS) in Paducah, Kentucky, in 1991. Since that time, I've continued to enjoy making Star quilts this way and have enjoyed teaching the process, because once students get the idea, they are pretty happy with the results. NORTHERN LIGHTS (page 24) by Eleanor Chamberland and STARGYLE (page 25) by Jean Impey are two examples made by students who have taken the idea and run with it.

Liberated Stars have become a feature in many of my quilts. I use them in samplers and frequently as corner squares. Keep your eyes open as you look through this book and you will certainly find them.

Seeing Stars

I've learned how to control the process to create stars that look almost as though they were made with templates and conventional piecing methods, or stars that are *very* Liberated. I like the idea that I can make both formal and less formal quilts with this process.

RIGHT: STARGYLE, detail. Made by Jean Impey and machine quilted by Nana's Capo Beach Quilting. Full quilt on page 25.

NORTHERN LIGHTS, 25" x 30½", 1996. Made and machine quilted by Eleanor Chamberland, Denver, CO.

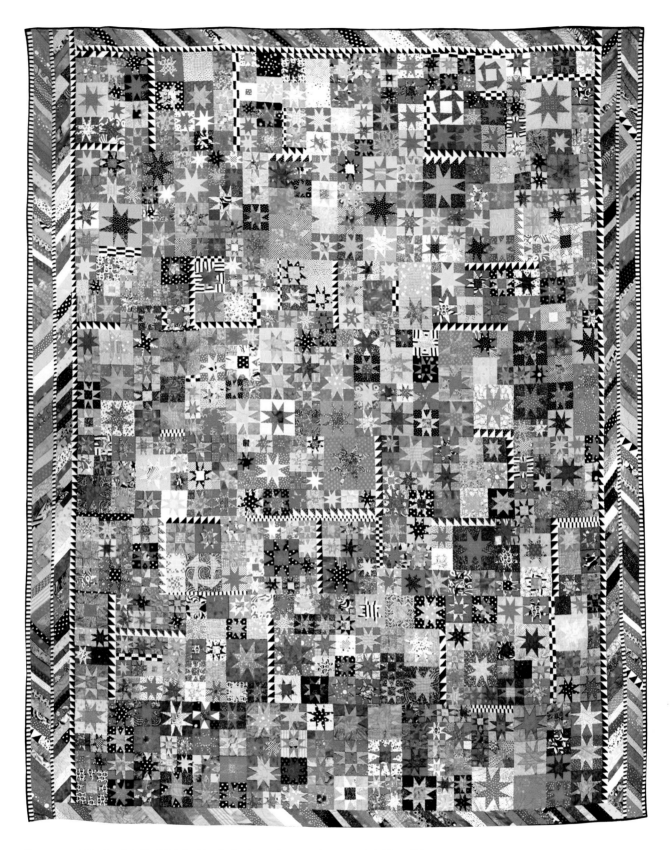

STARGYLE, 108" x 132", 2008. Made by Jean Impey, Corona del Mar, CA, and machine quilted by Nana's Capo Beach Quilting. PHOTO: JEAN IMPEY

You can see the informality of GWENNY'S VARIABLE STAR and GWENNY'S VARIABLE STAR WITH APPLIQUÉ BORDER (page 27). The points vary quite a bit and the colors are all mixed up. In GWENNY'S VARIABLE STAR I mixed up the colors of some of the star points and even included a small star in the center of one of the larger star blocks. These rather serendipitous elements add to the playful character of these two quilts.

GWENNY'S VARIABLE STAR, 56" x 66", 1995. Made and machine quilted by the author.

GWENNY'S VARIABLE STAR WITH APPLIQUÉ BORDER, 56" x 66", 1995. Made and hand quilted by the author.

Basic Concept

Free-piece star points onto a background square; this base square serves as a template to resize the unit.

A collection of sophisticated prints prompted the decision to make a more formal Star quilt: LIBERATED STARS (page 29). The blocks are set block-to-block but appear to float because the star points don't come to the very edges of the blocks.

Step-by-Step: Liberated Star Block

One quality that I like about Liberated Stars is that they fairly twinkle. That's because the star points vary. To help understand how this block goes together, look at my sample block below. This sample will serve as our map as we go through the steps together.

Seeing where you want to go makes the job of getting there much easier. Notice that this block is a Nine Patch. It's made of nine squares, four of which have star points. All you need to do is learn how to make the star-point units; the rest is easy to figure out.

Begin by choosing a background (base square) fabric and a fabric for the star points. The center square can be the same as the background, the same as the star points, or a different fabric altogether.

Sample Liberated Star block

Decide what size you want the finished block to be. The formula for cutting the base (and center) squares is the same for blocks of any size: add ½" to the finished size of each square (¼" on all four sides for seam allowance). For this lesson, we'll make the 6" finished star shown (left), so begin by cutting eight 2½" squares from the background fabric, and one 2½" square for the center square.

To make the star-point unit, here is what you'll do in a nutshell:

- Sew a triangle on the right side of the square, press, and trim.
- Sew a triangle on the left side of the base square, press, and trim.

Having said that, I've taught enough "star making" to know that lots of quilters initially have trouble figuring out how to place the triangle. Most people have to make a couple of Star blocks to understand how it works.

It's a perceptual problem, and it's harder for some people to see it than others, so let's go through it step-by-step.

LIBERATED STARS, 70" x 80", 2003. Made and hand quilted by the author.

There are three ways you can make Liberated star points: from half-square triangles, from elongated triangles, and from rectangles. Experiment to find the process that works best for you.

Making Star Points from Half-Square Triangles

The idea here is to cut the half-square triangles for the star points a little on the large side to make placement on the base square easier. Start by cutting four squares slightly larger than the base squares from the star-point fabric. (For the 2½" base squares in our sample block, I cut the star-point squares 3" x 3".) Next, cut each star-point square in half from corner to corner.

Figure 1 tells the whole story. This full-sized drawing can be your map as you make your first Star block. It shows the finished 2" unit, right-side up, surrounded by a ¼" seam allowance on all four sides; the position of the triangle, right-side down, on the right side of the square; and the stitching line. The colored triangular shape in the upper right-hand corner gives you an idea of what the finished star point will look like.

Once you've got the pieces cut, you're ready to start sewing.

1. Position a half-square triangle on the right side of four base squares as shown (fig. 1). Sew the triangles to the squares, chain piecing them if you like.

2. Press the unit, triangle-side up, making sure the base squares remain flat. Turn the unit over, square-side up, and trim the edges of the triangle even with the edges of the base squares (fig. 2).

3. This step is optional: If you wish, turn the unit back so that it is triangle-side up, flip the triangle out of the way, and trim the excess base square even with the raw edge of the triangle (fig. 3). Fold the triangle back into position and press (fig. 4). I've done it both ways (trimming or not); however, I definitely trim the base layer if I plan to hand quilt the star points and/or if the fabric seems a bit bulky.

4. Repeat steps 1–3 to add triangles to the left side of the base squares, press, and trim.

Figure 5 shows some star-point possibilities: points can overlap, be different lengths, have a space between, sit off center, or be chopped off at the tips.

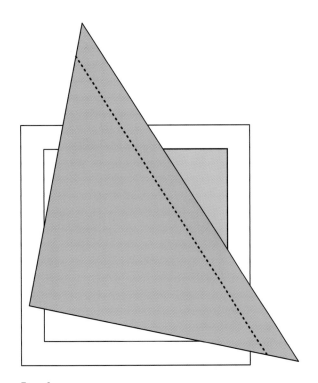

Fig. 1

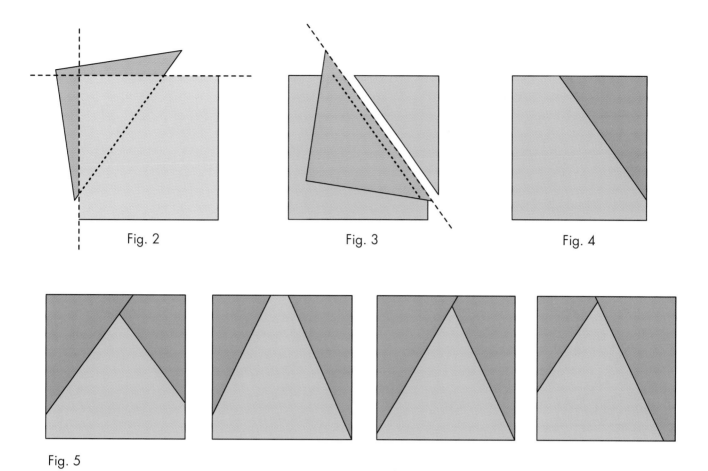

Fig. 2   Fig. 3   Fig. 4

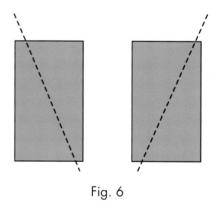

Fig. 5

Making Star Points from Elongated Triangles

Instead of squares, these star points are cut from rectangles, which are closer to the shape of the point and therefore can be easier to position. Notice that the cuts are not made exactly from corner to corner (fig. 6).

Run a test to determine how large to cut the rectangles. You can do this with paper. Cut a rectangle out of paper, and cut it diagonally to create two triangles. Position one triangle on the base square, and fold the triangle back to see if it is big enough to do the job.

Fig. 6

If you're using prints for the star points, you'll need to cut both left and right points.

Once you've cut the base squares and triangles, piece the elongated triangles to the squares following the steps in "Making Star Points from Half-Square Triangles" (page 30).

> If you layer two rectangles wrong sides together and cut, you will automatically get two sets of right and left star points. Do this two times, and you'll have enough points to make one Star block.

Whichever way you decide to make your star points, once you've learned the basic process, you can chain piece the units. Sew all the points to the right side of the base squares, press, and trim. Sew the points to the left side of the base squares, press, and trim. Then it's just a matter of arranging the four star-point units, the remaining background base squares, and the center square, and sewing the units and squares together.

Making Star Points from Rectangles

Making star points from rectangles works just fine too. Figure 7 shows the actual sizes of the pieces required for our 6" sample block so you can see how this method works. Run a little test to see what size works best for the size unit you want to make.

Base-Block Variations

Here are a few other easy ideas for using base-block construction:

Liberated Stars with Pieced Sashing

Another way to create Liberated Stars is to sew triangles to sashing, as I did in MORNING STAR (page 33). Take a close look at this quilt, and you'll see that it's made with plain, unpieced squares that have been set together with pieced sashing. It was easy: I stitched two Liberated star points at both ends of the rectangular sashing strips. Figure 8 shows how a Liberated Star appears at the junction of four blocks.

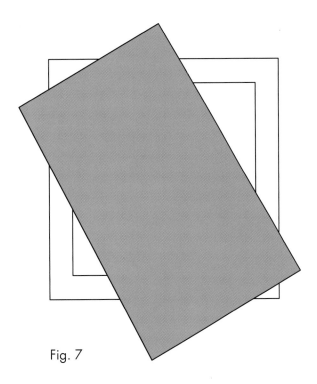

Fig. 7

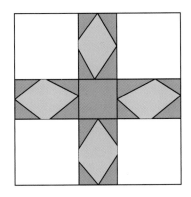

Fig. 8

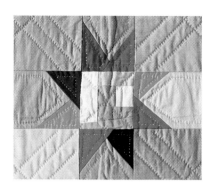

Knowing how to make Liberated Stars with sashing is very useful; you can sprinkle a few stars in *any* sashed quilt.

MORNING STAR displays a bit of playful inconsistency: some sashing strips along the outer edges of the quilt are missing triangles, and some of the center squares are pieced with Liberated compositions.

MORNING STAR, 42" x 51", 1996. Made and hand quilted by the author.

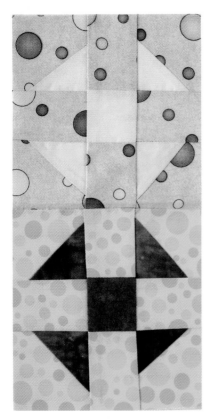

Liberated Shoo Fly

Liberated Shoo Fly Block

Liberated Shoo Fly blocks are made in very much the same way as Liberated Stars, except that you sew just one triangle to each of four base-block squares.

Take a look at my OLD McDONALD's SHOO FLY and Karen Setla's LIBERATED SHOO FLY (page 35) for examples of quilts using this variation.

OLD McDONALD's SHOO FLY, 58" x 64", 1992. Made and machine quilted by the author.

LIBERATED SHOO FLY, 77" x 92", 2004. Made and hand quilted by Karen
Setla, Bath, MI.

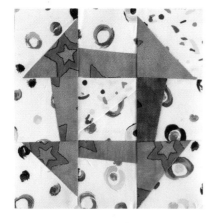

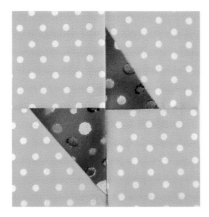

The Exquisite, Liberated Style

The Exquisite (page 37) is another block that can be made with the base-block construction process. If you know how to make Liberated Stars, you have little new to learn about making this block.

The Exquisite is aptly named. It's an old pattern listed as Number 281 in the *Ladies Art Company* catalog reprint from 1928. It appeared in its Liberated form in *Liberated Quiltmaking* (see Bibliography, page 125).

Recently, Debbie Trichler picked up the idea and made MACKENZIE'S QUILT (page 37) in classic red and white. Look carefully at this wonderful quilt, and you will see that the block consists of a base rectangle with triangles sewn to opposite corners. (Yes, this block can be made with a base square or a base rectangle.)

Here are a few other simple blocks you can make using what you've learned in this chapter: Liberated Churn Dash, Liberated Pinwheel Star, and Liberated Simple X.

RIGHT: LIBERATED LADY, 2008. Made by Judi Hasselkus, Mission Viejo, CA. Collection of the author.

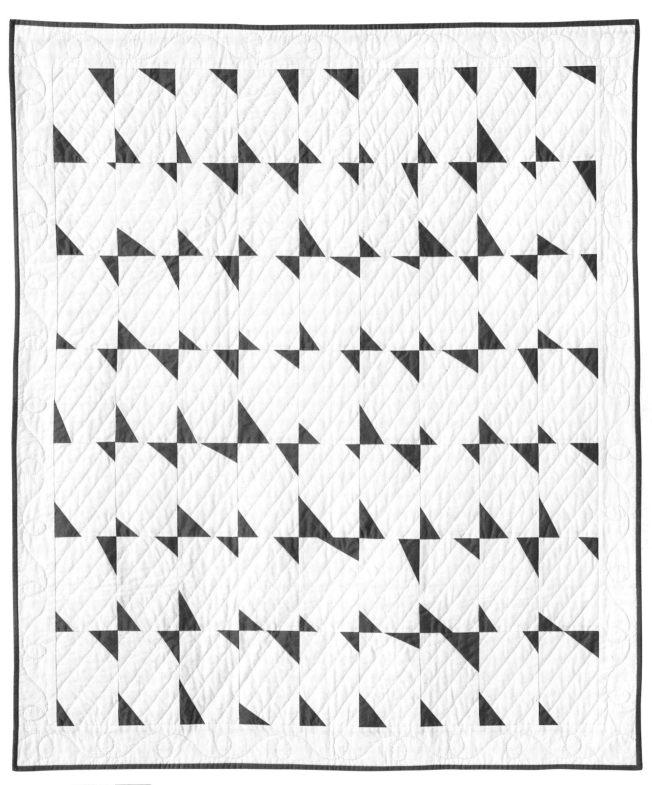

MACKENZIE'S QUILT, 45" x 46", 2009. Made and hand quilted by Debbie Trischler, Unionville, MI.

LEFT: The Exquisite block.

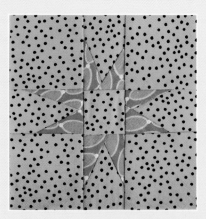

Play with the dimensions of the units and squares for interesting effects.

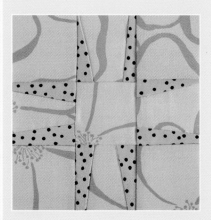

The Stick Star block

GWENNY'S VARIABLE STAR WITH APPLIQUÉ BORDER, detail. Full quilt on page 27. Note the little stars within the bigger Star blocks.

What If...

...you make the star points different colors?

...you decrease the width of the four star-point base squares and the size of the center square?

...you make the points narrow and fairly straight, resulting in what I call the Stick Star?

...you make the center square a Liberated composition of your own choosing?

...you pop a little Star in the center square, making a Star-Within-a-Star as I did in GWENNY'S VARIABLE STAR (page 26)?

Below are some additional star possibilities from the original *Liberated Quiltmaking* for your review (fig 9).

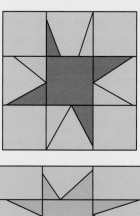

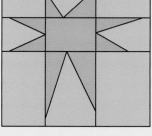

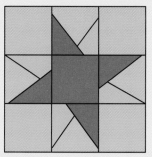

Fig. 9

PROCESS 3 : Kathy's Block

Kathy's Block

The year was 2002 and I was conducting my Beaver Island Quilt Retreats. The theme that year was "Old-Fashioned Samplers." Kathy Hogard was in her first year of attending my retreat, and—at one point—she asked me to show her how to make a Liberated Star. I did a quick demo to get her started, only to come back later and discover that my demo perhaps had been *too* quick. Kathy had a lot of units made, none of which were quite right.

Here is where the saying "making lemonade out of lemons" applies. That is exactly what Kathy did. Upon discovering the problem, she and I began playing with the blocks she'd made to see what we could do with them. Making Star blocks wasn't an option, but certainly we could come up with something that could be just as good—or maybe better.

In the end, Kathy's Block gave birth to many new ideas for which I and other students always give her credit. In fact, Kathy has gained a certain celebrity at my annual quilt retreats, which she retains to this day. It's a truly wonderful lesson to learn: When things don't turn out as expected, don't despair. Rather, see if there aren't some worthwhile possibilities hidden within. This is a good approach both to quiltmaking and to life in general. Many wonderful inventions have come from unexpected results.

KATHY'S BLOCK WITH SASHING, detail. Full quilt on page 40.

Let's Look at the Quilts

Kathy's Block is easy to make and can be set in any number of ways to create different outcomes. In KATHY'S BLOCK WITH SASHING, I made four-block, sashed units and then set them together with sashing and corner squares.

BELOW: KATHY'S BLOCK WITH SASHING. 34" x 42", 2002. Made and hand quilted by the author.

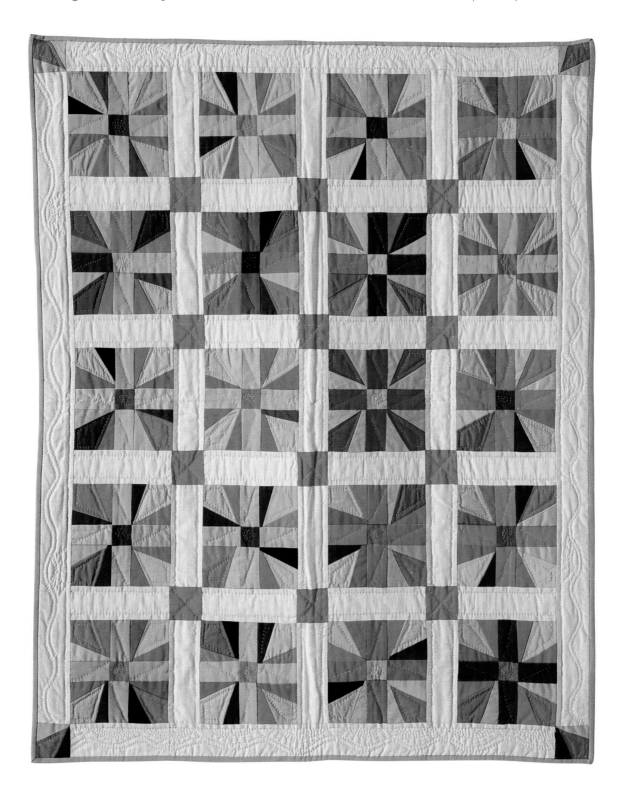

In THIS WAY AND THAT, I experimented with sewing nine blocks together and turning them "this way and that." In doing so, I fulfilled a longtime wish to make an entire quilt by letting the joined blocks go their own way.

THIS WAY AND THAT, 30" x 37", 2002. Made and hand quilted by the author.

In TULIPS FOR KATHY, I turned Kathy's Block into a tulip and arranged the blocks in a rather North-Carolina-Lily way. The larger block is put together as described for LIBERATED ROSE (page 91) in "Process 7: Liberated Square-Within-a-Square."

TULIPS FOR KATHY, 57" x 72", 2002. Made and hand quilted by the author.

Karen Griska attended my quilt retreat the same year that Kathy Hogard did, and she picked right up on Kathy's idea to make the wonderfully scrappy SERENDIPITY.

SERENDIPITY, 52" x 52", 2002. Made and machine quilted by Karen Griska, White Plains, NY. Collection of the author.

Cathy Jones flipped the units to create a very different look in LEONARD'S PASSING. Cathy was snowed in at her Beaver Island home when she got the news that her father had died. She was alone, in a blizzard, and unable to get out of her house, much less off the island to join her family. She spent the day making this lovely quilt in remembrance of her father.

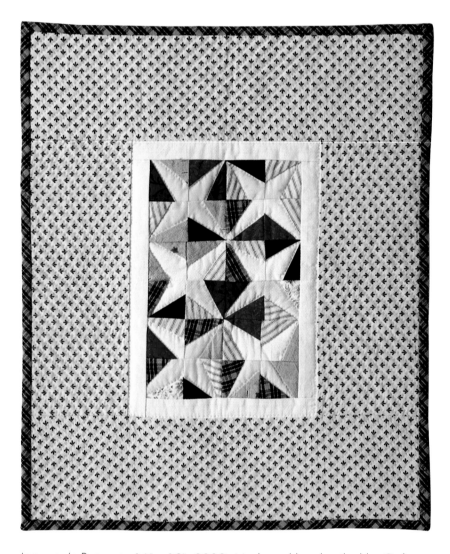

LEONARD'S PASSING, 16" x 19", 2002. Made and hand quilted by Cathy Jones, Beaver Island, MI, in memory of her father.

Basic Concept

The process for making Kathy's Block is similar to piecing Liberated star points. This time, free-piece triangles onto *two adjacent sides* of a base square so that the points meet in one corner rather than landing on opposite corners; the base square serves as the template to resize the block.

Step-by-Step: Kathy's Block

Let's begin by looking at the star-point unit required to make a Liberated Star block (fig. 1) and an example of Kathy's Block (fig. 2). You can see they are very similar, and it would be easy—with just a demo given on the run—to sew the second triangle in an ever-so-slightly different position.

In Kathy's Block, the two triangles meet *in the corner* and actually overlap a bit. I now have seen quite a number of quilts made with this block, and I can tell you that you don't need to worry about how much the triangles overlap. They can overlap a little bit or quite a bit, and they don't all need to overlap in the same way.

Since this block is made using the base-block method discussed in "Process 2: Base-Block Construction" (page 23), you might want to review that chapter before you begin.

As with the Liberated Star, the formula for cutting the base square is the same for blocks of any size: add ½" to the finished size of one square (¼" on all four sides for seam allowance). For this lesson, we'll make a 3½" finished block, so begin by cutting a 4" square from the base-square fabric. Next, cut two 3" x 5" rectangles from the fabric you want to use for the points.

> You might want to make a test block or two to determine if the measurements given work for you, or whether you want to alter them somewhat. For example, you might want to cut the side rectangles larger, or you might want to change the finished size of the block, in which case you'll need to experiment to determine what size to cut the side pieces.

1. Position one rectangle on the base square as shown, right sides together (fig. 3). Sew the rectangle to the square (fig. 4).

Fig. 1. Star-point unit

Fig. 2 Kathy's Block

Fig. 3

¼"

Fig. 4

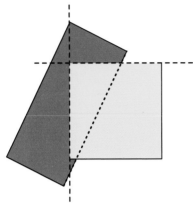

Fig. 5

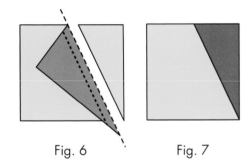

Fig. 6   Fig. 7

2. Press the unit, rectangle-side up, making sure the base square remains flat. Turn the unit over, square-side up, and trim the edges of the rectangle even with the edges of the base square (fig. 5).

3. While not essential, I think it best to trim the excess base fabric so there is less bulk where the points come together. (This is even more critical if you plan to hand quilt the finished top.) Turn the unit back so that it is triangle-side up, flip the triangle out of the way, and trim the excess base square even with the raw edge of the triangle (fig. 6). Fold the triangle back into position and press (fig.7).

4. Repeat steps 1–3 to add a rectangle to the adjacent side of the base square, press, and trim as shown in figure 8. (The "x" shows which side to sew the rectangle to.) The resulting triangles should overlap in the corner.

Fig. 8

An alternative method to cut the side pieces is to cut a rectangle, and then cut the rectangle in half diagonally, not quite corner-to-corner, to make two elongated triangles. Refer to "Making Star Points from Elongated Triangles" (page 31) for guidance. *(Remember: You need to cut left and right triangles for each block.)*

What If...

...you sew four blocks together and set them block-to-block? The seams within the blocks won't line up for an even more Liberated look, and the four blocks create a secondary design at the point where they meet.

MEXICAN HAT DANCE, detail. Full quilt on page 47. Notice the Liberated "joins" and secondary pattern where the blocks meet.

MEXICAN HAT DANCE, 40" x 47", 2008. Made and hand quilted by the author.

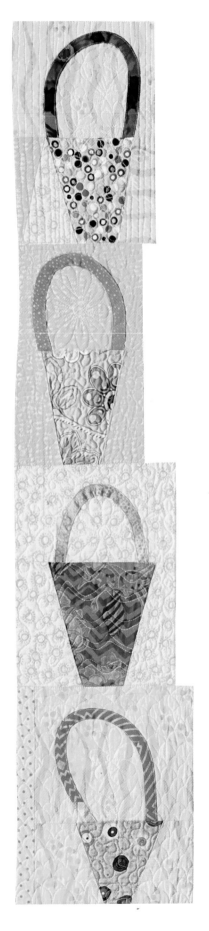

P R O C E S S 4: Liberated Baskets

I made my first Liberated Basket quilt in 1992 and have been experimenting with this process ever since. There are many possible shapes to explore, and—depending on your fabric choices—your baskets might take on a sweet look, an arty look, a playful look, or a traditional look. As with all Liberated ideas, you can work in a more controlled or a less controlled way to create either a formal or informal quilt.

Let's Look at the Quilts

Let's take a moment and review the Basket quilts shown in this chapter. You'll see a lot of variations. Look carefully and you'll notice that the handles are "where the action is."

In Gwenny's Baskets in Pastels (page 49), the backgrounds are a mix of mostly yellow prints, with a few greens tossed in for flavor. The basket shapes vary widely in shape. A few are pieced with leftovers from other baskets, and the handles differ radically. The finished blocks are consistent in size vertically, but different in width so they don't line up horizontally. I'll tell you how that works in a little bit.

LEFT: Gwenny's Baskets in Pastels, detail

OPPOSITE: Gwenny's Baskets in Pastels, 59" x 73", 2006. Made by the author and machine quilted by Robyn House.

SAND PAILS is similar to GWENNY'S BASKETS IN PASTELS (page 49), in the way the blocks were made, but the basket shape has been altered slightly to more closely resemble a sand pail. The fabrics were specifically chosen to reinforce the beach theme. (Note: Finding the right fabrics requires a trip to Florida in March.)

BELOW: SAND PAILS, 60" x 74", 2007. Made by the author and machine quilted by Robyn House.

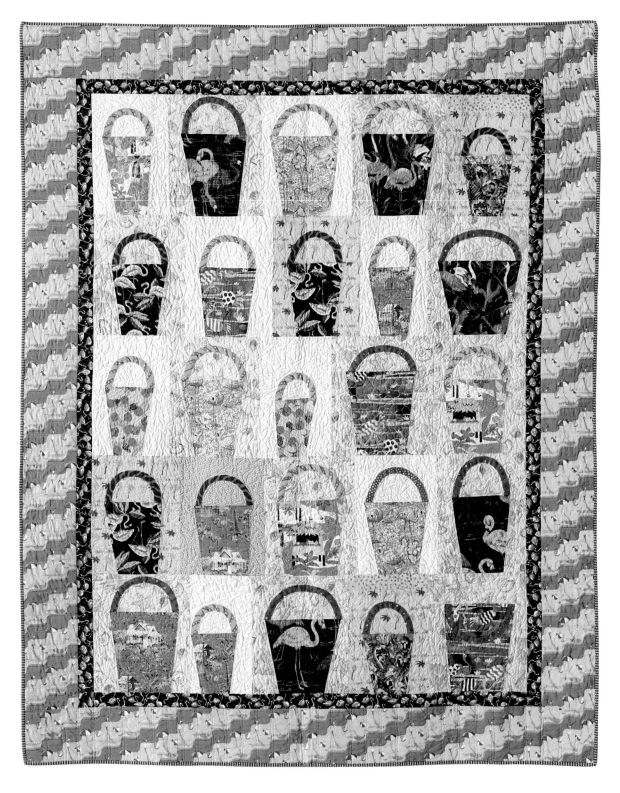

In my view, BASKETS FOR OLIVE ROSE has a bold and lively look. It is yet another basket shape to work with, and I think the use of red and blue contributes to the quilt's rather sassy character. The prints are from a fabric line called Olive Rose designed by Valori Wells of The Stitchin' Post (Sisters, OR) fame.

BELOW: BASKETS FOR OLIVE ROSE, 51" x 62", 2009. Made by the author and machine quilted by Robyn House. This quilt was made with fabrics designed by Valori Wells of The Stitchin' Post, Sisters, OR.

The theme of my 2007 Beaver Island Quilt Retreat was "Basket Quilts," so in this chapter, you'll find four of the many sensational quilts made that year. For example, in her quilt I CAN HANDLE IT, Pam Foster took basket handles to new heights to create a playful, eye-catching quilt. As you study this quilt, don't miss Pam's use of rickrack and the creative filler strips she used to make the rows fit together.

BELOW: I CAN HANDLE IT, 30" x 42", 2007. Made and machine quilted by Pam Foster, Muskegon, MI.

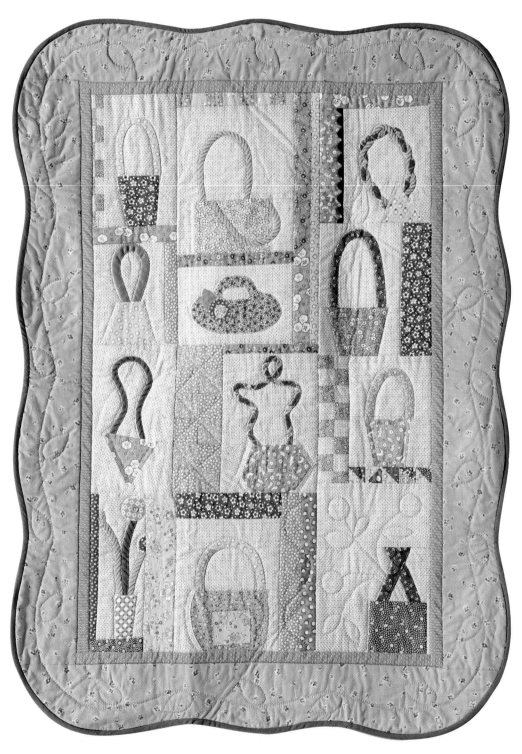

Cathy Jones discovered lots of basket shapes, and managed to get them all sewn together into one quilt, which she titled DANCING BASKETS. The icing on the cake is her delightful, quite traditional border and the lovely hand quilting, which she did on her full-sized quilting frame.

BELOW: DANCING BASKETS, 64½" x 76", 2007. Made and hand quilted by Cathy Jones, Beaver Island, MI.

BELOW: LIBERATED BASKET, 74" x 92", 2007. Made and hand quilted by Karen Setla, Bath, MI, as a gift for Pam McCabe.

For LIBERATED BASKET, Karen Setla began with a beautiful selection of fabrics, used a simple basket base, garnished the baskets with cherries, and made an exciting quilt topped off with beautifully hand-quilted fans.

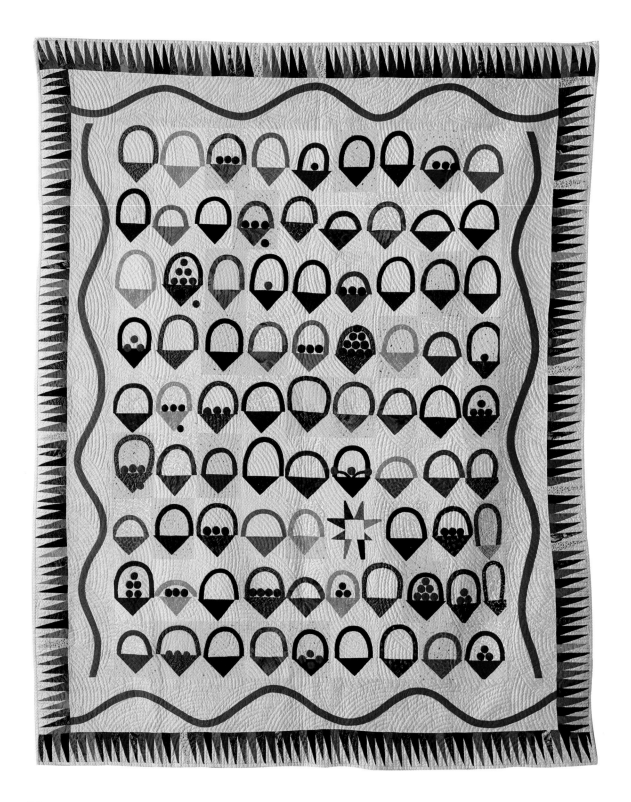

Joyce Harlan made CLAYTON'S QUILT for a special little grandson. Clayton, we learned, was especially alert to birdsongs, and urged anyone nearby to "hear the bird." We all loved watching Joyce work on her quilt—and what a charming quilt it is. Notice that she decided to put handles on the borders. A real breakthrough there!

BELOW: CLAYTON'S QUILT, 54" x 50", 2007. Made and machine quilted by Joyce Harlan, Birmingham, MI, for her grandson.

Basic Concept

Make this block in two major sections. Free-piece the basket section. The handle section can be free-pieced or appliquéd.

When it comes to Liberated Baskets, the action is in the handles!

What we all learned about making Liberated Baskets is that there are a great many options. Begin with a seed of an idea, make a little sketch, and—if it will help you—make a full-sized sketch as well. Figure out the most practical construction procedures, and then get started, making any changes (artistically and technically) that occur to you as you work. That's how it goes in the world of Liberated Quiltmaking, and that is how you, Dear Reader, will get your very own, original Basket quilt.

Step-by-Step: Liberated Basket Block

In the following pages, I'll tell you how to make the block in Gwenny's Baskets in Pastels (page 49) and how to adapt the method to make the Baskets for Olive Rose (page 51) block. Once you've mastered these techniques, you'll be ready to try your own unique variations. The options are endless.

Gwenny's Baskets in Pastels Block

I made these blocks all the same height, but in different widths.

Making the Basket Section

1. Cut a strip of background fabric 11" x 42" (the width of the fabric). Using your quilter's ruler *as a straight edge only*—remember, this is Liberated Quiltmaking—eyeball and cut segments of different widths ranging from about 5½"–8" wide (fig. 1).

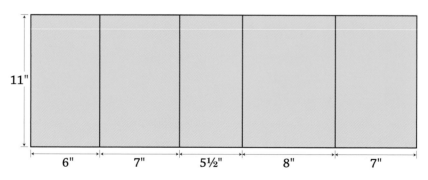

11"

6"   7"   5½"   8"   7"

Fig. 1

2. From the fabrics you've selected for the baskets, cut simple basket shapes by eye.

3. Position a basket shape on a background segment and cut along the top of the basket shape as indicated by the dashed line (fig. 2). Set the top "half" of the background piece aside for now.

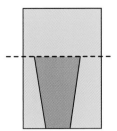

Fig. 2

4. With both pieces right-side up, place the basket shape on the bottom "half" of the background piece. Shift the basket slightly to the right, and cut along the left side of basket shape as shown by the dashed line (fig. 3). Repeat, this time shifting the basket shape to the left, and cutting along the right side of the basket (fig. 4).

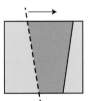

Fig. 3

5. Sew the trimmed-off left and right background pieces to the basket shape, completing the lower section of the block. You'll quickly discover that this pieced lower section is now larger than the top piece you set aside in step 3. The solution is to add on to the top section, or to trim down the bottom section you've just completed.

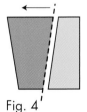

Fig. 4

Making the Handle Section

After making a fair number of Basket quilts myself, and then seeing what the 150 or so quilters produced at my quilt retreats in 2007, it became apparent that the action in these Liberated Basket blocks is in the handles. The work goes easily using my slick method for making and sewing bias on by machine.

If you decide to make the top piece wider, you can use the same background fabric, or choose a different fabric for a scrappier look. If you look closely at GWENNY'S BASKETS IN PASTELS (page 49), you'll see that the latter is exactly the choice I made in some of the blocks.

RIGHT: GWENNY'S BASKETS IN PASTELS, detail. Full quilt on page 49. For some blocks, I added on to the top background piece with a different fabric for an even scrappier look.

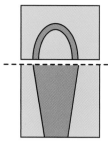

Fig. 5

> To avoid pinning the handle to the ironing board, slip a 6" x 12" ruler under the handle section before pinning.

> If you enjoy hand appliqué, you can use that method to stitch the handles to the background.

1. For bias that finishes ½" wide, cut bias strips 1¼" wide.

2. Set your sewing machine for the longest stitch: the basting stitch. Turn both long raw edges inward to the wrong side of the strip, overlapping them slightly, and sew down the center of the strip. (You'll remove the basting stitches once the handle is stitched to the block).

3. Place the basket section and top section on your ironing board so you can position the bias handle to line up with the basket as you wish (fig. 5). Position the handle by pulling it gently with your left hand and following with a hot iron guided by your right hand. Pressing the curve this way helps eliminate any tucks or puckers.

4. Leave both sections on the ironing board as you pin the handle in place. Place the pins perpendicular to the handle.

5. Set your sewing machine to make a small stitch; I use #12 on my Singer® Featherweight. Beginning with the *inside* curve, sew the handle to the background piece by stitching just inside the handle's edge. Continue across the short end of the handle and sew the outside edge to the background in the same fashion. You can use matching or contrasting thread. I usually choose one color and use it for sewing down all the handles.

6. Remove the basting stitches and press. Sew the two sections of the block together, press, and straighten the edges of the block.

Assembling Uneven Rows

1. Arrange the blocks in a visually pleasing manner, and in a way that makes the horizontal rows about the same length. Since the blocks are different widths, this is like working out a jigsaw puzzle, and just as much fun. Do what makes the most sense. Add more fabric here and there and/or cut off fabric here and there to make it work.

2. Sew the blocks together in horizontal rows, sew the rows together, and border as you like.

A Basket Variation: Baskets for Olive Rose Block

A little different basket shape requires a little different process. For this variation, I began by making a rough, full-sized sketch to get an idea of scale and to determine the most practical way to construct the block. I cut the basket shapes about the same height and in slightly different shapes, all by eye.

This basket shape required a side piece of background on the top left and right sides of the basket, and also on the bottom left and right sides. I decided the easiest way to attach these side pieces was to cut strips of the background fabric. My rough sketch informed me approximately how wide to cut the strips. I also placed the basket shapes on the background fabric, which helped me to verify these measurements.

1. With both pieces right-side up, place a basket shape on a strip of background fabric. Cut along the bottom angle of the basket, and the top angle if necessary (fig. 6). Repeat to cut the bottom left background piece.

2. Sew the trimmed-off background pieces to the bottom right and left angles of the basket shape. Press and trim as necessary.

3. Repeat steps 1 and 2 to cut and sew the top background pieces to the top right and left angles of the basket shape (fig. 7). Press and trim.

4. Make and attach the handle using the technique described in "Making the Handle Section" (pages 57–58).

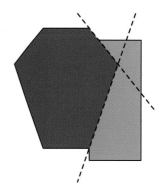

Fig. 6

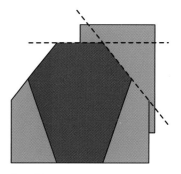

Fig. 7

It's easy to add rickrack to the handles. Tack the rickrack in place by stitching down the center. Position the bias handle over the rickrack so that the edge of the rickrack peeks out on one side, and then stitch the handle in place.

As an alternative, choose rickrack wider than the finished bias handle (e.g., wider than ¼"), and center the handle so that the rickrack peeks out from both sides.

RIGHT: BASKETS FOR OLIVE ROSE, detail. Full quilt on page 51. Rickrack adds a playful detail to the handle of this Basket block.

What If...

...you make the baskets with food fabrics? A basket of cherries sounds nice.

...you cut the top of your basket at a slight angle in a few blocks?

...you piece the basket itself and/or handle sections in Liberated fashion?

...you make the sides of your baskets curved—and the appliquéd handles angled?

...the handle of your basket runs right off the edge, as in the block below, made by Jean Howe?

...you make a single Liberated Basket block and finish the edges with satin stitch, as Lois Griffith did in the example below right?

Both baskets and handles can be pieced Liberated style.

Mix up the shapes of your baskets and handles.

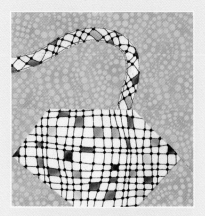

Liberated Basket block made by Jean Howe, Kentfield, CA

LEFT: BASKET, 4" x 6", 2008. Made by Lois Griffith, Columbus, IN. Wouldn't this make a lovely postcard, gift tag, or little gift for someone special?

5: Liberated Triangles: Sawtooth Borders and Wild Goose Chase

I've rarely started a border without being tempted to make it a Sawtooth border...and very often I haven't been able to resist temptation! I argue with myself, saying I should do some *other* kind of border, but—nevertheless—I come back to my old favorite Sawtooth. Why? Because I think a Sawtooth border has a classic look that just can't be beat. That said, I now introduce you to the Liberated Sawtooth border, made—of course—with Liberated Triangles.

Working with Liberated Triangles is especially freeing because of the variations you can get and the punch these triangles can add to your quilt. It's also one of the Liberated methods that makes the point that "Liberated" doesn't necessarily mean "faster." In the case of Liberated Triangles, the process is actually slower and more complicated than piecing the "traditional" way.

So why would you want to make triangles the Liberated way? *Because they are worth the little bit of extra effort!*

LORRAINE'S MEDALLION, detail. Full quilt on page 101. The center panel of this medallion-style quilt is framed by a colorful Liberated Blunt-Nosed Sawtooth border.

Frankly, I don't have a problem with the process being a bit slower. To my mind, in the quilt world today, there is way too much talk about "fast and easy," "quick and easy," "quilt in half a day." Since we all love making quilts, why the rush to get it over with as quickly as possible? Enjoying the process is such an important part of making a quilt, and things that are worth doing just might take longer than half a day. I *love* sewing, so I'm not trying—first and foremost—to "get it over with." I'm not trying to wrap it up so I can go off and dust.

Let's Look at the Quilts

Let's take a moment to look at the quilts in this chapter and examine the Sawtooth variations in them.

SAWTOOTH, 43" x 49", 2009. Made and hand quilted by the author.

My entire SAWTOOTH quilt (page 62) is made from a shape that I've seen used by African-American quilters and have heard referred to simply as Sawtooth. In trying to differentiate between the three types of Liberated Sawtooth border variations in this chapter, I've named this version Blunt-Nosed Sawtooth. You'll see I've also used the Blunt-Nosed Sawtooth as the outermost border of CHECKERBOARD MEDALLION WITH SAWTOOTH BORDERS, below, and on LORRAINE'S MEDALLION (page 101), which is shown in "Process 8: Liberated Medallions."

This blunt-nosed variation appeals to me because of its boldness. There isn't much difference in the size and shape of the triangles, and the fact that the angles are quite similar makes this version the easiest of these triangle variations to make.

BELOW: CHECKERBOARD MEDALLION WITH SAWTOOTH BORDERS, 37" x 38", 2009. Made and hand quilted by the author.

In addition to the Blunt-Nosed Sawtooth border, CHECKER-BOARD MEDALLION WITH SAWTOOTH BORDERS (page 63) features another Sawtooth variation similar to the border on QUILT WITH LIBERATED SAWTOOTH BORDER as shown below. The shapes in these borders are closest to equilateral triangles, so I think of them as Liberated Equilateral Triangles.

ABOVE: QUILT WITH LIBERATED SAWTOOTH BORDER, 45" x 46", 2009. Made and hand quilted by the author. Fabrics hand dyed by Kathy Swanteck.

LEFT: QUILT WITH LIBERATED SAWTOOTH BORDER, detail. I refer to the triangles that make up the Sawtooth border in this quilt as Liberated Equilateral Triangles.

The third Liberated Sawtooth variation is the spiky version of my quilt FRAMED RED SQUARES II (page 82), which appears in "Process 6: Recut Blocks and Recut Sashing." The Liberated Spiky Sawtooth is probably the most dramatic of them all, and—in a red-and- green color pairing—it *really* vibrates. In certain light, it's actually hard to look at; it's so powerful, that it's distracting. I've made this spiky version in other color combinations and it's still dramatic, but much softer than in this color duo.

In the following pages, I'll suggest several methods for making these wildly wonderful, free-pieced triangle borders; however, as you work, you'll naturally find your own approach, and that's as it should be.

Liberated Sawtooth Fundamentals

You'll note that all the quilts shown in this chapter are made with solids, and that's a point to consider when you're constructing borders with odd-sized triangles. Solids don't have a "right" and "wrong" side as prints do, and this can be a critical difference. I'll explain how the process works with solids first, if it applies, and then explain what needs to happen if you choose to work with prints.

There are three steps that apply to all three Liberated Sawtooth variations.

■ Before you begin cutting, make a test drawing of what you want to make. You'll use this as your map.

■ Choose the colors (lights and darks) you want to use and cut strips of fabric the height you want the triangle to be plus ½" for seam allowance.

■ When the border is assembled, press, and then straighten the long edges.

> ### Basic Concept
> Cut odd-sized triangles in contrasting colors or values and sew them together. In order to fit together, the touching sides of adjacent (neighboring) triangles must be cut at the same angle.

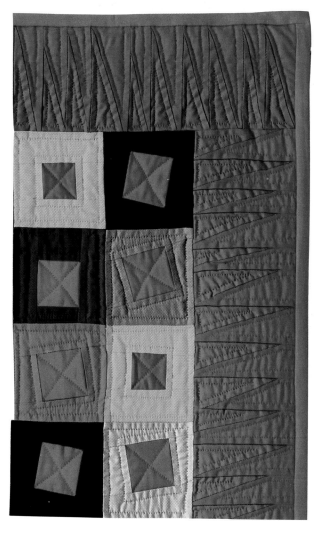

FRAMED RED SQUARES II, detail. Full quilt on page 82. The intense red/green color combination in this Liberated Spiky Sawtooth border gives added power to this already dynamic quilt.

Step-by-Step: Liberated Blunt-Nosed Sawtooth

Good news! My process for making this Sawtooth version is the same whether I'm working with solid fabrics or prints. This version is easy to make because the angles are very similar; the sizes of the triangles change, but the angles vary only slightly. It might help you to take a look again at the two quilts that show the Liberated Blunt-Nosed Sawtooth (CHECKERBOARD MEDALLION WITH SAWTOOTH BORDERS, page 63, and LORRAINE'S MEDALLION, page 101).

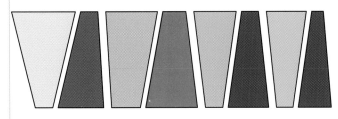

Fig. 1

1. Before you begin cutting, make a test drawing of what you want to make to use as your map.

2. Choose the colors (lights and darks) that you want to use, and cut strips of fabric the finished height you want the triangle to be plus ½" for seam allowance.

Fig. 2

3. Using a rotary ruler and rotary cutter, cut triangle shapes by eye, keeping the angles very similar, but varying the width somewhat. You'll want to see how the process works before cutting all the shapes, so cut just enough to get started.

4. Arrange a row of eight to 10 triangles, right-side up, in an order (colors and shapes) that appeals to you (fig. 1). If you have the triangles lined up neatly, you can see that most of them will fit together, meaning that the sides that are touching are the same or very close to the same angle.

Fig. 3

5. Touching triangles with angles that *aren't* the same will need to be recut so that the angles match. Keeping the pieces right-sides up, pivot the smaller triangle around and place it on top of the larger triangle, keeping the top and bottom edges straight. Recut the angles so they are the same (fig. 2), pivot the smaller triangle into its original position, and sew the two triangles together (fig. 3).

6. Continue adding triangles as described in the steps above. When you've completed the row, press and straighten the long edges, as they are likely to be a bit uneven (fig. 4).

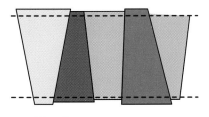

Fig. 4

Step-by-Step: Liberated Equilateral Sawtooth

Let's start with how this process works for solid fabrics. I'll explain how to adapt it for prints on page 68.

1. Before you begin cutting, make a test drawing of what you want to make to use as your map.

2. Choose the colors (lights and darks) that you want to use, and cut strips of fabric the finished height you want the triangle to be plus ½" for seam allowance.

3. Cut an "equilateral" triangle by eye from one fabric, and place the triangle, right-side up, on a strip in a contrasting color. Cut along the left edge of the triangle as indicated by the dashed line (fig. 5).

4. Sew the cutaway end piece to the triangle (fig. 6) and you are ready to begin building your border by adding alternating light and dark triangles.

5. Place the triangle unit, right-side up, on a strip in a contrasting color. Cut along the right edge of the triangle as indicated by the dashed line (fig. 7). Toss the corner piece away.

6. Pivot the unit around, and sew the triangle unit to the angled strip (fig. 8).

7. Cut an angle on the strip as shown by the dashed line (fig. 9). Now you have two triangles sewn together.

> I sew the triangle onto the strip first, and then cut the angle because if I don't, I'm very likely to pick up the triangle, and turn it the wrong way before I get to the sewing machine. Since these "nearly" equilateral triangles look pretty much the same on all three sides, it's an easy mistake to make.

> You can make the triangles similar in size and shape, or you can make them radically different.

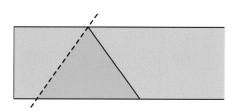

Fig. 5

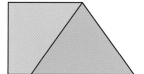

Fig. 6

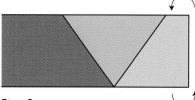

Fig. 7

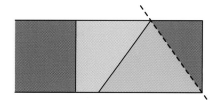

Fig. 8

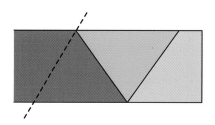

Fig. 9

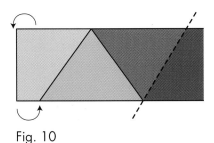

Fig. 10

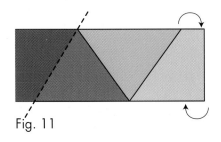

Fig. 11

If your strip isn't angled in the same direction as the triangle, turn the strip over. Presto! This works with solids only—because solids don't have a right and wrong side.

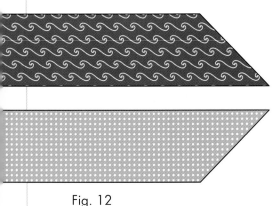

Fig. 12

8. Pivot the unit around, place it—right-side up—on a contrasting strip, and cut the angle (fig. 10). Pivot the unit and sew it to the strip (fig. 11).

9. Continue cutting and adding triangles as described in the previous steps. When you've completed the row, press and straighten the long edges, as they are likely to be a bit uneven.

Adapting the Liberated Equilateral Sawtooth for Prints

Working with prints is a bit different because these fabrics have a right and wrong side. Therefore, if the strip is angled in the wrong direction, you can't turn the strip over and use the other side. Each triangle requires a triangle in a contrasting color on both its right and its left sides, and the right-side angle goes in a different direction than the left-side angle.

There is no way to make a strip angled one way fit a triangle that is angled in the other direction. The easiest solution is to cut strips of both lights and darks with angles going in both directions. That way, whatever side you are adding to, there will be a strip heading the right way (fig. 12).

Another way to make both the Blunt-Nosed Sawtooth and the Liberated Equilateral variation is to employ the currently popular method of layering four to six strips of fabric, cutting the angles, and rearranging the units to fit. While perhaps easier, the results aren't as interesting to me because the outcome appears predictable, repeating the same colors and the same shapes. It works, but in my view, not as well. I like watching the border grow and being able to decide what color should come next, and what shape it should be. Again, I have found that there are more important things in both art and life than "quick and easy."

Step-by-Step: Liberated Spiky Sawtooth

This is actually a base-block construction process, so knowing that up front will make these instructions easier to comprehend. It might be helpful for you to flip back to "Process 2: Base-Block Construction" (page 23) for a quick refresher course before you start sewing. As is usual with this method, the base block will serve as your template for trimming.

You can make your Liberated Spiky Sawtooth units look the same or you can make the lengths vary, depending on the effect you want to achieve. You also can chain piece these units, which speeds up the process considerably.

1. Before you begin cutting, make a test drawing of what you want to make to use as your map.

2. Choose the colors (lights and darks) you want to use, and cut strips of fabric the finished height you want the triangle to be plus ½" for seam allowance.

3. Decide what the background color(s) will be and what color(s) you'll be using for the Spiky Sawtooth pieces. Cut a background strip by eye into slightly different-sized segments (fig. 13).

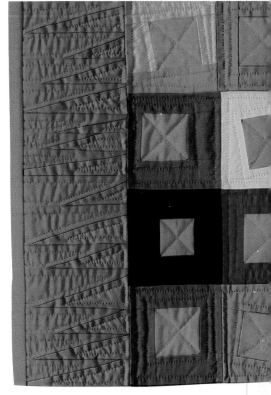

FRAMED RED SQUARES II, detail. Full quilt page 82. Example of a Spiky Sawtooth border.

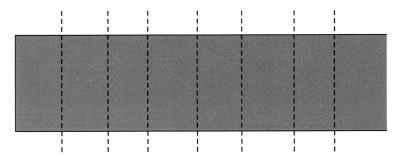

Fig. 13

4. For the sawtooth pieces, cut rectangles from a sawtooth strip a bit wider than the background segments you cut in step 3. Cut just a few at first to see if they are the right size. You don't want them too big or too small. You want them to be "just right," which means big enough to place easily on the base (background) block.

5. Place the sawtooth rectangle on the base block, right-sides together, making sure that—when folded back—the sawtooth rectangle completely covers the corner of the base block. Sew the pieces together (fig. 14).

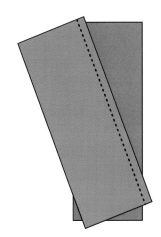

Fig. 14

6. Flip the sawtooth rectangle back and press, keeping the base block flat (fig. 15).

7. Turn the unit over, base-side up, and trim the edges of the sawtooth rectangle even with the edges of the base block (fig. 16).

8. Because I planned to hand quilt my quilt, I trimmed the excess base block ¼" beyond the seam to reduce the bulk (fig. 17). Figure 18 shows the finished unit.

9. Continue making Spiky Sawtooth units as described in the previous steps. When you've completed the row, press and straighten the long edges, as they are likely to be a bit uneven.

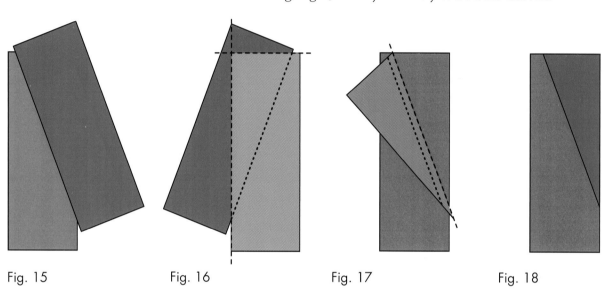

Fig. 15   Fig. 16   Fig. 17   Fig. 18

WILD GOOSE CHASE, detail. Full quilt on page 71. While I varied their shapes a bit, I kept the geese consistent in height and width in this quilt.

Liberated Wild Goose Chase: Five Ways

Wild Goose Chase is one of the classic quilt patterns that quilters return to over and over again. Often the blocks are sewn into vertical rows that are joined to create an entire quilt. This is the way WILD GOOSE CHASE (page 71) was made. Sometimes the rows are separated by wholecloth strips, and sometimes Wild Goose Chase borders are used to frame a quilt.

In my collection, I have an amazing antique Wild Goose Chase quilt from Maine. What makes this old quilt unique is the scale of the individual units, which measure 16" wide x 8" high. I don't ever remember seeing another Wild Goose Chase quilt with such large geese. It seemed like a great idea when I was planning my WILD GOOSE CHASE.

The units in WILD GOOSE CHASE measure 12" wide x 6" high. I used different yellow background fabrics and a variety of splashy prints for the geese.

There is always more than one way to make any Liberated block, and that is certainly true with Wild Geese. You can control the process for a more formal look, or ease up on the control for a more free-spirited look.

Notice that the geese in WILD GOOSE CHASE vary somewhat in *shape* from block to block, but are consistent in width and height. This gives the quilt a more controlled look. Changing the height and width of the geese results in a looser, more informal look, as you can see in MEDALLION WITH WILD GEESE AND SQUARES ON POINT (page 102).

BELOW: WILD GOOSE CHASE, 60" x 74", 2009. Made by the author and machine quilted by Robyn House.

Medallion with Wild Geese and Squares on Point, detail. Full quilt on page 102. Geese in varying heights and widths result in a more "radical" look.

Here are five different ways to make Liberated Wild Geese, most using ideas touched on in other sections of this book. Within each process, the method for cutting and constructing the units differs a bit, as do the results. That is the glory of Liberated Quiltmaking: Your Wild Geese can choose how they are going to fly! Read through all five methods, and pick the one that seems best to fit the way you like to work.

In all of these methods, you can cut the goose (larger) triangles the same width, but at different angles, or cut them completely by eye so that they are different widths, different heights, and different angles. You can run a test to check your "vision" by drawing a full-sized section of four or five geese to get a sense of their scale and shape, and also make a paper test to determine how big to cut the side pieces. Again I remind you to cut *some*, but not *all*, of the pieces before you start to sew. You may want to make adjustments once you get started and see how it's going.

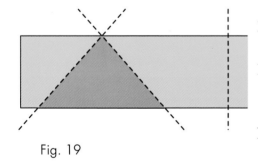

Fig. 19

Fig. 20

METHOD 1: Easiest, but Wasteful

This method is similar to the method I described in "Making the Basket Section" in "Process 4: Liberated Baskets" (page 48).

1. Cut one strip each of two contrasting fabrics in matching heights—one for the goose and the other for the background.

2. Cut a large goose triangle by eye. With both pieces same-side up, place the goose triangle on the background strip. Cut along both sides of the triangle, and then cut a straight edge to separate the unit from the background strip, allowing enough to square up the unit later (fig. 19).

3. Sew the two background pieces to the goose triangle, and press (fig. 20).

METHOD 2: Double-Cutting

This method works well if you are making blocks with a variety of background fabrics, but not if you are using a single background fabric for all the blocks. The method is the same as "Method 1: Easiest, But Wasteful" (page 72), except that the two fabrics are layered and cut at the same time, so there isn't any waste. Each layered pair of fabrics yields two Wild Geese units.

1. Cut two rectangles of contrasting fabrics to the width and height you want the finished units to be, plus ½" in both directions (width and height) for seam allowance.

2. Layer the pieces same-side up, and cut the goose triangle by eye, starting at least ¼" in from both the left and right bottom corners (fig. 21).

3. Separate the geese and the side (background) pieces. Sew two contrasting background pieces to each goose, and press (fig. 22).

The units need to finish the same width in order to fit together in vertical rows.

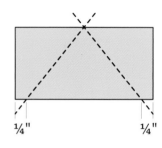

¼"   ¼"

Fig. 21

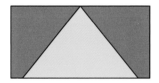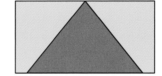

Fig. 22

METHOD 3: Working with Strips

You can use this method with either solids or prints, but the instructions on page 72 are specific to prints. It is less complicated if you use solids because solids don't have a right and wrong side, and you can just turn the background strip over and the angled end will be reversed. (Try it once, and you'll see how it works.) Still, to be a well-rounded Liberated Quilter, you need to know how to accomplish this with either solids or prints.

This method may seem a little confusing at first—because it is. Trust me: Once you get into it, you'll be fine. Follow the instructions carefully to see how it works; you'll also probably find what doesn't work as well.

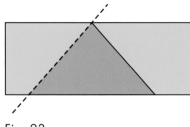

Fig. 23

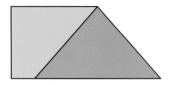

Fig. 24

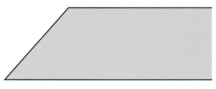

Fig. 25

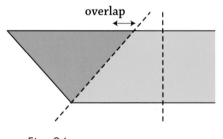

Fig. 26

1. Let's cut the side triangles for the left sides first. Cut some large geese triangles by eye. Cut a strip of background fabric wide enough to accommodate the height of the geese triangles.

2. With right-sides up, place a goose triangle on the background and cut the left-side angle as indicated by the dashed line (fig. 23). Sew the trimmed background piece to the triangle, and press (fig. 24). The trimmed end of the remaining background strip will resemble figure 25.

3. To cut the left-side piece for another goose triangle, turn the triangle upside down and place it, right-side up, over the angled end of the angled background strip. If you free-cut your triangles, the angled edges probably will not match exactly, so the trick is to extend the angled edge of the triangle slightly beyond the angled end of the strip. Recut the angle using the triangle as a guide, and then cut a straight edge to separate the unit from the background strip, allowing enough to square up the unit later (fig. 26).

4. Sew the trimmed background piece to the triangle, and turn the unit so that the base of the goose triangle is at the bottom; the new unit will look just like the unit you pieced in step 2. In other words, the left-side pieces will be complete.

5. Continue the process described above, cutting all the left-side pieces from the same strip of fabric, and then repeat the process to cut and piece the right-side pieces.

METHOD 4: Working with Triangles

This method works for both solids and prints.

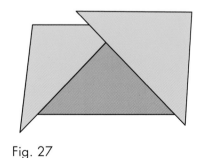

Fig. 27

1. Cut some large geese triangles by eye.

2. Cut squares into oversized half-square triangles for the side pieces. As is usual with Liberated techniques, this requires a little experimentation to determine how large to cut the squares so the side triangles are large enough. Once you've figured that out, you can cut a bunch of half-square triangles, and chain piece them onto the geese (fig. 27).

3. Once you've made the desired number of units, press, straighten all edges, and trim to the same width so that they can be joined into rows (fig. 28).

> K eep in mind that you will eventually sew the units into rows; cut the pieces so the units can be trimmed to the same width.

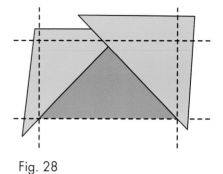

Fig. 28

METHOD 5: Base-Block Construction

If you tried the techniques in "Process 2: Base-Block Construction" (page 23), "Process 3: Kathy's Block" (page 39), or even some of the options described in this chapter, this method should seem pretty familiar by now.

1. For the base blocks, cut rectangles to the finished size you want the unit to be, plus ½" in both directions (width and height) for seam allowance. For a more free-spirited look, vary the height from block to block.

2. Cut oversized rectangles for the side pieces. (You can use oversized triangles if you prefer.) These pieces must be large enough to cover the base-block rectangle, so I recommend that you run a little test with paper to determine how large to cut them.

3. Place a side rectangle, right-sides together, with a base-block rectangle as shown in figure 29. Stitch as indicated by the dotted line.

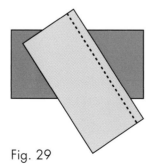

Fig. 29

RIGHT: I used rectangles and the base-block construction method to make this Liberated Wild Goose Chase sample.

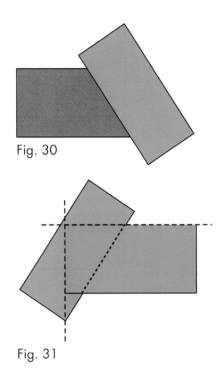

Fig. 30

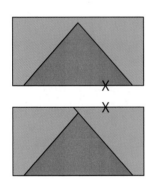

Fig. 31

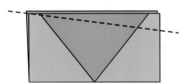

Fig. 32

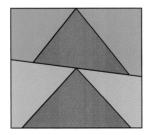

Fig. 33

Fig. 34

4. Flip the stitched rectangle back and press, making sure that the corner of the base rectangle remains flat (fig. 30).

5. Turn the unit over, base-rectangle-side up, and trim the edges of the side rectangle even with the edges of the base rectangle (fig. 31).

As with all base-block construction, you have the option to trim—or not to trim—the excess base-rectangle fabric to leave a ¼" seam allowance. When constructing Liberated Wild Goose Chase units, however, I think trimming away the excess fabric is best, and here's why. In a quilt such as WILD GOOSE CHASE (page 71) the rows of geese are sewn right next to each other to make a vertical row, so it helps to reduce the bulk by trimming the extra layer of fabric. Otherwise, you'll be sewing through four layers of fabric, not two. The problem multiplies as you sew the rows side by side, matching the horizontal seams. There are some things about conventional piecing that make sense, and this is one place where I think that applies.

6. Repeat steps 3–5 to add a background rectangle to the remaining short side of the base rectangle, press, and trim.

Sewing Units Together with Angled Seams

Look again at my WILD GOOSE CHASE sample (page 71) and at LIBERATED FLYING GEESE by Biz Storms (page 77). Notice the skewed seams between some of the geese. In both cases, angling the seams adds another interesting design element which, when introduced even sparingly, can enliven the whole.

1. Study figure 32. To angle the seam between two units, you must cut the bottom edge of one unit at an angle identical to the top edge of the second unit. I've indicated each edge in question with an "x."

2. Pivot the top unit around so the edges that need to be identical are lined up with each other, right-side up. Cut at an angle (fig. 33).

3. Sew the two units together and press (fig. 34).

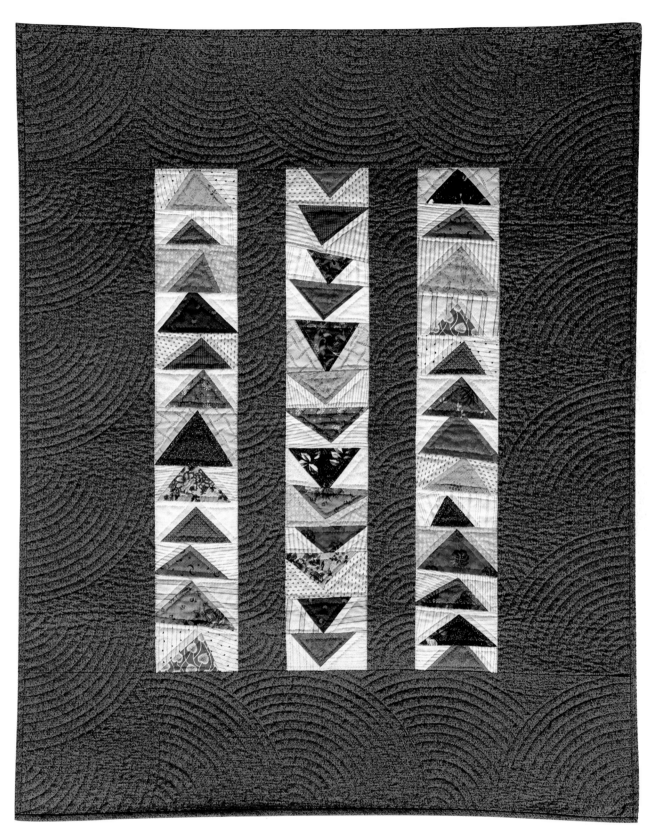

LIBERATED FLYING GEESE, 36" x 44", 2001. Made and hand quilted by Biz
Storms, Toronto, Canada.

What If...

...the author (me) became so partial to these Liberated Sawtooth ideas, that when I started working on this chapter, I stopped writing and started sewing, turning my first "what if" into the LIBERATED SAWTOOTH IN BARS quilt shown below? That's exactly what happened!

...you switch the colors (or values) of the geese and the backgrounds in some of the Wild Geese units?

...you sew rows of Liberated Wild Geese into pairs, and then separate these with a wider plain bar? Once you have the rows made, play with them in different arrangements. For example, switch some of the rows from top to bottom, so the geese change direction. You won't be disappointed.

BELOW: LIBERATED SAWTOOTH IN BARS, 41" x 44", 2009. Made and hand quilted by the author. This quilt is a take-off on the classic pattern Tree Everlasting.

6 ∘ Recut Blocks and Recut Sashing

TUMBLING JACKS, 40" x 52", 2009. Designed and pieced by Charlotte Hase. Quilted by Cindye Baily.

R ecutting is a wonderful way to give traditional blocks a distinctive—and Liberated—new look. It works with certain blocks, but not all. Obviously recutting a Feathered Star block wouldn't be a good choice. In general, simple blocks are more likely to work best.

GWENNY'S OWN NINE PATCH (page 80) was my first experiment with recut blocks. I made it early in 1992 using reproduction prints. I quilted it in allover fans, signed and dated it in the quilting, bound it with a single-fold binding cut on the straight grain, as is my custom, and put it on my bed. To make a quilt like this you need only to understand the basic concept and several simple construction tips which apply to all recut blocks.

Here are two planning strategies that apply to all recut blocks:
◾ If you are uncertain how big to make the oversized block so that it is large enough to recut easily, draw the block full size, and then draw in the lines for recutting the block. This is a surefire way to see if the oversized block will be sufficient for your desired result (fig. 1).

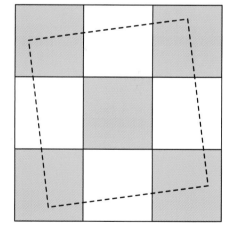

Fig. 1

Basic Concept
Make an oversized block in the desired pattern. Place your square ruler at an angle on top of the oversized square, and recut to the desired size.

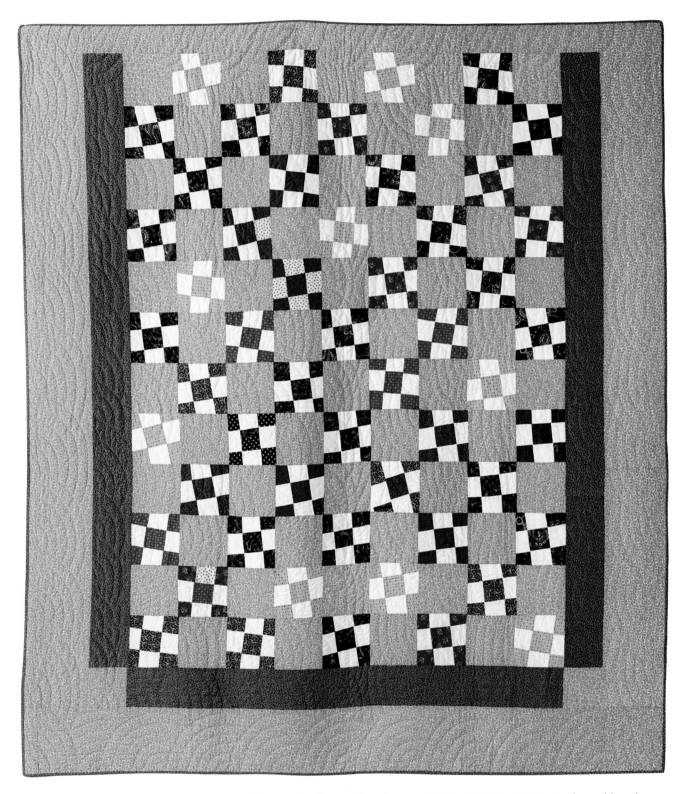

GWENNY'S OWN NINE PATCH, 67½" x 73½", 1992. Made and hand quilted by the author.

▪ Cut a piece of paper to the desired finished size of the recut block plus seam allowances, and use it as a template. The template makes it easier to cut the block because you don't need to read all four points on the square ruler to make sure the ruler is positioned correctly.

That's pretty much all you need to know to understand the basics for making recut blocks. The following instructions explain some specifics about how the recut blocks in this chapter were made. You'll find other possibilities to explore in "What If..." (page 89) at the end of the chapter.

Step-by-Step: Recut Framed Red Squares Block

The finished size of the block in FRAMED RED SQUARES II (page 82) is 4" square.

Since I did not recut these blocks at a radical angle, I found that a 5½" block was large enough to recut to 4½", which includes the necessary ¼" seam allowances.

Keep in mind: As I am writing about a process rather than describing how to make a specific project, it is not my intention to give you the exact measurements to duplicate my quilt. Rather, I am showing you how to figure out how to make your own blocks any size you want. You can do this easily by making a test drawing as I did (fig. 2). The drawing tells you everything you need to know: How large to make the block so that it can be recut, and how wide to cut the strips that frame the different-sized "red" squares. You will want to oversize the strips enough so you can recut the block easily.

If you are interested in the dramatic border on this quilt, refer to "Step-by-Step: Liberated Spiky Sawtooth" (page 69).

1. Based on your drawing, cut a "squarish" shape for the block center, and four oversized strips for the frame.

2. Sew the strips Courthouse Steps Log-Cabin style around the block center, pressing as you go.

3. Place a square ruler at an angle on the block and trim to size. Remember to include the ¼" seam allowance on all sides.

FRAMED RED SQUARES II, detail. Full quilt on page 82.

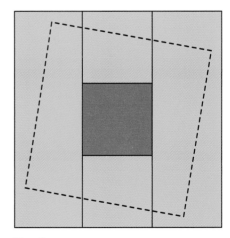

Fig. 2

FRAMED RED SQUARES II, 41" x 45", 2009. Made and hand quilted by the author.

Step-by-Step: Jacks Block

This quilt was included on page 165 in *Liberated Quiltmaking* where it was called Pinwheels. I had this quilt with me at my 2008 Beaver Island Quilt Retreat, and the quilters all seemed to think it looked like children's jacks. They began calling it Jacks and the name stuck. I've always thought this quilt had a playful quality about it. It also reminds me of a box of crayons.

Sample Recut Jacks block

Here is a sample block and the recipe to make it. This block finishes 4½" square, but you can alter any aspect of the block as I did. In my quilt, I changed the width of the colored strips and mixed the colors in some of the blocks.

Don't cut all the strips at first. Cut some and see how the process works and how you like the outcome. You may decide that the block is slightly easier to recut if you don't make it quite so large to begin with. You'll make more informed decisions after you've made a few blocks.

1. To make one 4½" finished block, cut a 3" x 16" white strip and a 1¼" x 16" colored strip. Sew the strips together to make a strip-set, and press toward the white.

2. Cut the strip-set into four 3¾" squares (fig. 3).

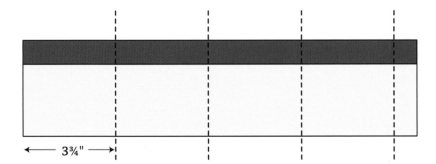

◄— 3¾" —►

Fig. 3

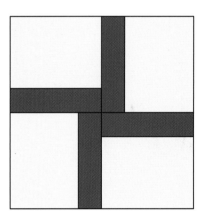

Fig. 4

3. Arrange the squares in two rows of two squares each. Sew into rows; press. Sew the rows together, lining up the center seam; press (fig. 4).

4. Place a square ruler at an angle on the block and recut into a 5" square (fig. 5). The block will finish 4½" square when sewn into your quilt.

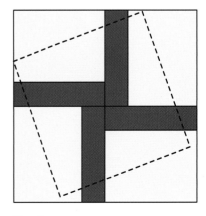

Fig. 5

JACKS, 48" x 66", 1993. Made and hand quilted by the author.

WINDMILLS, 50" x 60", 1999. Made and hand quilted by the author.

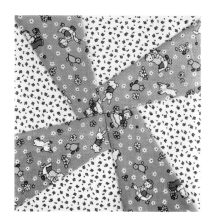

Sample Recut WINDMILLS block

Step-by-Step: WINDMILLS Block

WINDMILLS (page 85) has a less radical look than some Liberated quilts. The units that make up the blocks are just slightly different, so the variations are not immediately noticeable. I used color substitution in some of the blocks, which gives the quilt a scrappier look.

The fundamental principle involved in making this block is that the angles to be joined must be *identical;* therefore, layer the print fabric and the background fabric on top of each other, *same-side* up, and then cut the angle. This same process is covered in "Process 5: Liberated Triangles: Sawtooth Borders and Wild Goose Chase" (page 61).

1. For each block, cut two 5" prints and two 5" background squares. Layer the squares on top of each other, same-side up. Working by eye, cut the layered squares at an angle (fig. 6). Now you have four print and four background pieces cut with the identical angle.

2. Sew a print and background piece together; press (fig. 7). Make four.

3. Arrange the units in two rows of two units each. Sew into rows; press. Sew the rows together, lining up the center seams; press (fig. 8). The outside edges of the block will be uneven because of the seams taken in piecing the units together.

4. Place a square ruler at an angle on the block and recut into a 7½" square (fig. 9). The block will finish 7" square when sewn into your quilt.

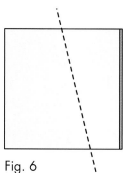

Fig. 6

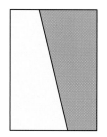

Fig. 7. Make 4.

Υou can vary the angle of the cut from block to block.

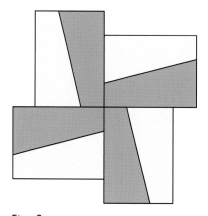

Fig. 8

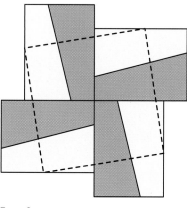

Fig. 9

SHOO FLY WITH RECUT SASHING, 54" x 66", 1993. Made by the author
and hand quilted by the late Sally Goodin.

Framing a Block with Recut Sashing

Recut sashing is a Liberated technique that offers a plethora of options. Sashing can be added to *any* block, and then the block recut for a skewed result. In SHOO FLY WITH RECUT SASHING (page 87), I added sashing in a high contrast fabric to two sides of a traditional block, sashing in the background fabric to the remaining two sides, and then angled my square ruler to recut the block. As a result, the block seems to dance.

You could, of course, cut all four sashing pieces from the same fabric. If you cut from the background fabric, the blocks appear to float, tipping this way and that.

By the way: Over the years, I've heard the words sashing and lattice used interchangeably. Just recently I found out that many quilters in North Carolina call it "stripping."

For this sample, I started with a relatively tame Liberated Log Cabin block, and framed the block with wide enough strips so that I could position my square ruler and recut the block at an angle.

What If...

...you experiment with re-cutting a string-pieced Kaleidoscope block (fig. 10)?

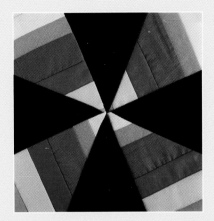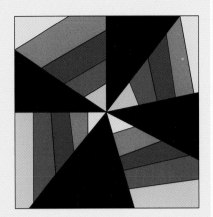

String-pieced Kaleidoscope block

...Here are some others you can try.

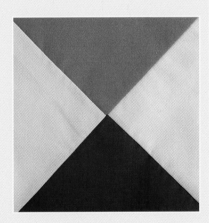

Nine-Patch Variation block

Pinwheel block

Hourglass block

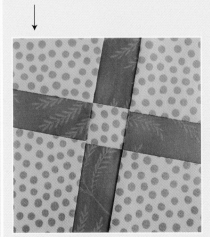

Recut Nine-Patch Variation block

Recut Pinwheel blocks

Recut Hourglass blocks

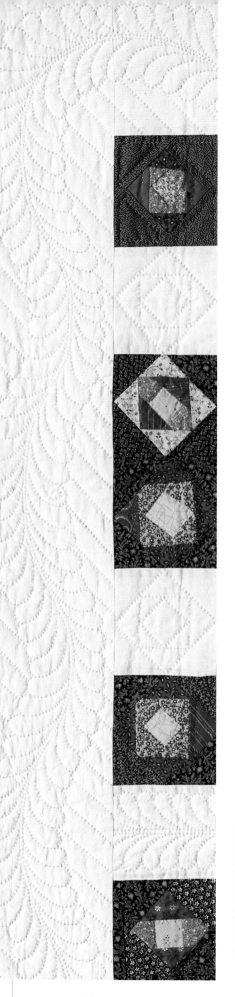

7. Liberated Square-Within-a-Square

Square-Within-a-Square is one of those traditional patterns that quilters and artisans worldwide have used for centuries. Walk through a few churches in Italy, and you're sure to see this familiar pattern beneath your feet. Its longevity affirms that it has proven itself to be good design.

I feel confident when I choose to work with a design like this. Because it has already passed the test of time, I know that I am starting with a solid idea. That is certainly no guarantee that my work will be successful, but I think it enhances my chances, and that is not only comforting, it's also just plain smart.

Each block begins with an odd-sized square that can vary from block to block. You can go around the center square once, twice, thrice, or more. In SQUARE WITHIN A SQUARE IN SOLIDS (page 93), I went around the center square once. I added two rounds of triangles in CABBAGES AND ROSES (page 92), and three rounds in LIBERATED ROSE (page 91). These three quilts, though similar, look very different due to the number of rounds, the scale of the block, and the fabric choices.

CABBAGES AND ROSES, page 92, and SQUARE WITHIN A SQUARE IN SOLIDS, page 93, clearly exemplify one of the main differences I see between working with prints and working with solids. Busy prints, especially with low contrast, tend to blur the line been the shapes, whereas solids emphasize the delineation. The effect of each is conspicuous in these two quilts.

Let's Look at the Quilts

One of my personal favorite styles of quilts is the four-block appliqué style popularized in the mid-1800s. As I was exploring Liberated pieced ideas, it occurred to me that I could replicate the four-block floral appliqués by using Liberated pieced units to replace the appliquéd flowers. The result was LIBERATED ROSE, made with small blocks in circa-1875 fabrics and set in a traditional four-block format.

BELOW AND OPPOSITE: LIBERATED ROSE, 64" x 64", 1997. Made and hand quilted by the author.

BELOW: CABBAGES AND ROSES, 50"
x 55", 2009. Made by the author
and machine quilted by Robyn
House. This quilt was made from
delicious prints designed by Kaffe
Fassett.

CABBAGES AND ROSES is made with a slightly larger block and pieced with contemporary prints. Here the scrumptious fabrics designed by Kaffe Fassett create a garden landscape with no effort at all. I went around the center squares twice, and stayed with the same fabric for each round.

SQUARE WITHIN A SQUARE IN SOLIDS is the simplest block, with the largest shapes. The solid fabrics push this quilt towards the art quilt category. In this quilt, the color of both the squares and the triangles is inconsistent, and therefore less predictable. What I like about this block is that—while simple—it is at the same time bursting with possibilities, which I find incredibly appealing. I think you'll agree. Once you begin to work with it, you undoubtedly will come up with other possibilities.

BELOW: SQUARE WITHIN A SQUARE IN SOLIDS, 38" x 38", 2009. Made and hand quilted by the author.

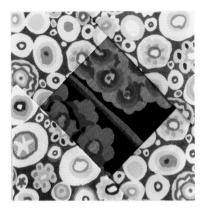

A basic Square-Within-a-Square block

The Basic Concept

Free-cut squares in different sizes. Cut side triangles oversized so that ultimately blocks can be trimmed to the same size.

Step-by-Step:
Basic Liberated Square-Within-a-Square Block

As I've recommended in many of the previous chapters, it is easy to see how to figure out what size squares and triangles to cut. Draw the finished size of what you want to make. This will serve as your guide, your map.

If you start out with different-sized squares, you can draw a different map for each one. Beginning with different-sized squares means all the other pieces will change in size too, and the blocks will look different.

1. Free-cut a "squarish" shape for the center square.

2. Using your map, cut two squares into four half-square triangles to make the first round of oversized triangles.

3. Sew triangles to opposite side of the square, and press (fig. 1). Trim the dog ears (fig. 2).

4. Sew the remaining two triangles to the remaining sides of the center square. Press, and straighten the block edges (fig. 3).

5. Repeat steps 2–4 to add additional rounds of triangles if desired.

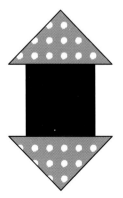

Fig. 1

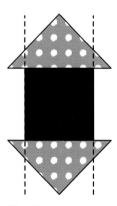

Fig. 2

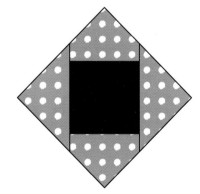

Fig. 3

Step-by-Step: LIBERATED ROSE Block

Here are the basic instructions for how I made the blocks for LIBERATED ROSE (page 91). Remember, however, that these are "Liberated" measurements and you are free to make adjustments.

This quilt is made with four large (24" finished) blocks, each consisting of four smaller (12" finished) blocks (fig. 4). Each 12" block includes three Liberated Square-Within-a-Square blocks. Each of these Square-Within-a-Square blocks finishes 4".

Instructions are for one 12" block.

1. Referring to "Step-by-Step: Basic Liberated Square-Within-a-Square Block" (page 94), make three Liberated Square-Within-a-Square blocks that measure 4½" unfinished, and that include three rounds of triangles.

2. For the large square with stems and leaves, cut an 8½" square. Use your favorite method for making and attaching bias, or refer to "Making the Handle Section" (page 57) in "Process 4: Liberated Baskets." Free-cut diamond-shaped leaves, place them by eye, and appliqué them.

3. Cut one 3" square in half once diagonally and sew one resulting half-square triangle to the corner of the block (fig. 5).

4. Arrange the three square-within-a-square units, the 8½" stem-and-leaf unit, and two 4½" background squares as shown in figure 4. Sew the units and squares together, pressing as you go.

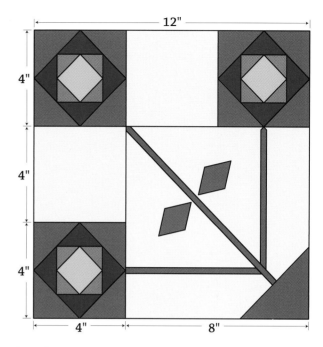

Fig. 4

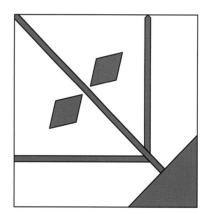

Fig. 5

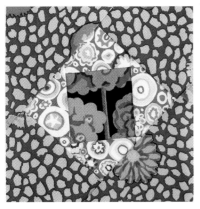

Sample CABBAGES AND ROSES block

Step-by-Step: CABBAGES AND ROSES Block

1. Free-cut a "squarish" shape somewhere between 2" and 3".

2. Cut two 3" squares into four half-square triangles to make the first round of oversized triangles.

3. Sew triangles to opposite sides of the square, and press (fig. 6). Trim the dog ears (fig. 7).

4. Sew triangles to remaining sides, press, and straighten the edges of the block (fig. 8).

5. Cut two 4" squares into four half-square triangles to make the second round of oversized triangles.

6. Repeat steps 3 and 4 to sew the second round of triangles to the unit. Press and trim the blocks to 5½" (fig. 9).

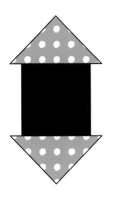

Fig. 6

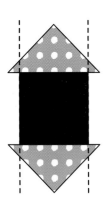

Fig. 7

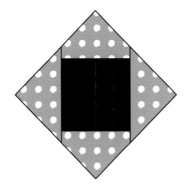

Fig. 8

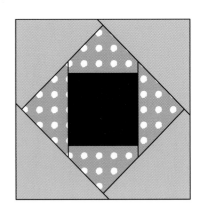

Fig. 9

Step-by-Step: Squares-on-Point Border

If you study my quilt MEDALLION WITH WILD GEESE AND SQUARES ON POINT (page 102), you'll notice that this quilt includes a border with elements that appear similar to the Basic Liberated Square-Within-a-Square block, but it's made in a different—faster—way.

The finished border in this quilt measures about 3½" wide. If you need or prefer a border of a different width, draw up a test segment on paper. This drawing will inform you as to what size to cut the parts.

The key is to cut the side triangles large enough so that you are able to trim the border edges even once the units are sewn together.

1. By eye, free-cut squares that measure from 1¾" square to 2½" square. These don't need to be exact squares as long as they appear "squarish."

2. Cut 5" squares, and then cut them diagonally in both directions to make four quarter-square triangles.

MEDALLION WITH WILD GEESE AND SQUARES ON POINT, detail. Full quilt on page 102.

To ensure that the edges of the border are on the straight grain and not on the bias, cut the triangles so that the long diagonal edge of each triangle is on the straight of the goods. These triangles need to be on the large side so they can be trimmed to size once the border is pieced. For the border in MEDALLION WITH WILD GEESE AND SQUARES ON POINT (page 102) I experimented on paper, and decided that triangles measuring 3½" on the short sides would work, and cut one triangle to that size. The long, diagonal edge measured 5", so I cut a 5" square, which I then cut on the diagonal in both directions (fig. 10). This gave me four triangles in the size I needed, with the long diagonal edge on the straight grain.

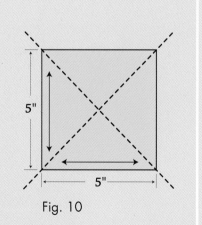

Fig. 10

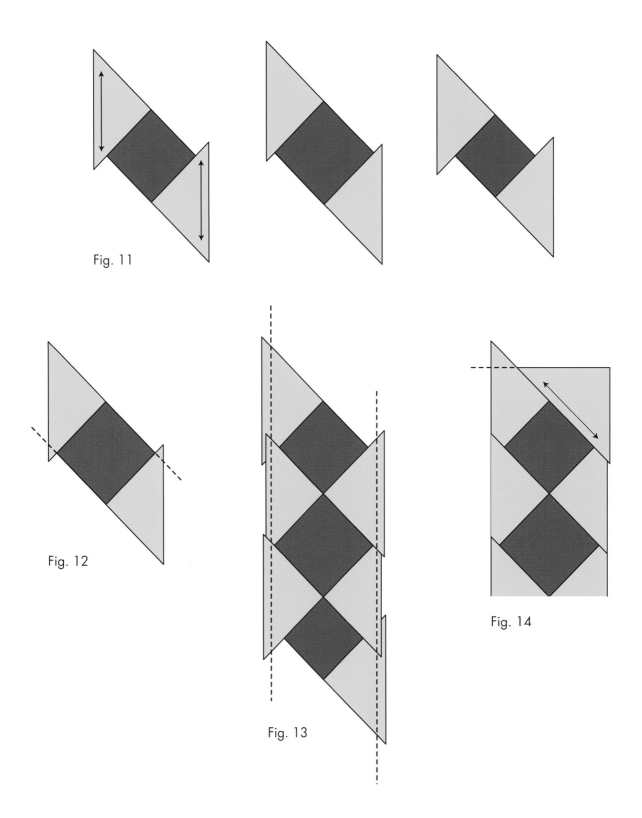

Fig. 11

Fig. 12

Fig. 13

Fig. 14

3. Sew a triangle to opposite sides of a square or squarish shape that you cut in step 1 (fig. 11). Place the triangles carefully. If you position and then piece them all incorrectly, you won't be happy. Press and trim (fig. 12).

4. Stagger the units and sew them together to make a border strip (fig. 13). Because the square shapes that you started with are slightly different in size, the edges of the border won't line up exactly, but they can be trimmed evenly once the units are sewn together. Press and straighten the border edges.

5. To finish off the top and bottom of the border strip, sew the *long diagonal edge* of a triangle to the first and last square or rectangle (fig. 14). This provides extra background at both ends, giving you the ability to trim the border to fit.

I find it helpful to make one unit and keep it next to my sewing machine for reference.

I find it easiest to sew and press the individual units into pairs, and then to sew the pairs into groups of four, and so on, rather than building a long border strip, unit by unit.

What If...

...you frame the center square in a high-contrast color to give it added emphasis?

...you make a variety of these blocks in different sizes and use them to make a Liberated Square-Within-a-Square sampler?

PROCESS 8: Liberated Medallions

Medallion quilts are one of the earliest styles of quilts made in America. Martha Washington was very familiar with this type of quilt; two of her medallion quilts belong to the Mount Vernon Ladies' Association and are shown in *Quilts of Virginia, 1607–1899: The Birth of America Through the Eye of a Needle* (see Bibliography, page 125).

Early medallion quilts began with a center area of interest, often a prized piece of fabric. The design built outward from the center panel in a series of borders—some pieced, some plain. Some medallions were rather simple in construction while others were heavily pieced.

All five medallion quilts shown in this chapter were made using some Liberated techniques. They were chosen to demonstrate that Liberated techniques can be used to create both contemporary-looking and traditional quilts. (Remember: It was my study of antique quilts that initially encouraged me to explore Liberated work.) Note that both the traditional Bits and Pieces (page 106) and the more contemporary-looking Lorraine's Medallion (page 101) make good use of Liberated Stars as cornerstones in the borders.

Let's Look at the Quilts

Lorraine's Medallion (page 101) and Medallion with Wild Geese and Squares on Point (page 102) have a contemporary look, while the other three quilts are as traditional as you can get. Let's take a close look at each one of these quilts to see what each is made of.

Lorraine's Medallion, detail. Full quilt on page 101. Liberated Star blocks grace the corners of two borders in this vibrant quilt.

LORRAINE'S MEDALLION, 51" x 59", 2002. Made by the author and machine quilted by Robyn House.

MEDALLION WITH WILD GEESE AND SQUARES ON POINT, 45" x 45", 2009.
Made by the author and machine quilted by Robyn House.

OPPOSITE: MEDALLION WITH WILD GEESE AND SQUARES ON POINT, detail

I was inspired to make LORRAINE'S MEDALLION (page 101) by the acquisition of a wonderful new line of fabric designed by Lorraine Torrence. (Thank you, Lorraine!) The sophisticated design of the fabric, coupled with the richness of its color, seemed like a sure bet to yield a strong quilt, and—in actuality—the fabric did much of the work for me. In fact, the center panel and four of the borders are cut as single, wholecloth pieces. There are only two pieced borders. The first is a Liberated Sawtooth border with Liberated Star blocks in the corners. (Stars show up again in the blue wholecloth border.) The second pieced border is a very traditional, conventional Square-Within-a-Square.

My choice of fabric for the center panel of MEDALLION WITH WILD GEESE AND SQUARES ON POINT (page 102) certainly informed my selections for the remaining fabrics of this quilt. The recipe here was simple: begin with a bold center fabric, and surround it with Liberated Wild Geese and Liberated Squares-on-Point borders. Instructions for the Liberated Wild Geese border can be found in "Process 5: Liberated Triangles: Sawtooth Borders and Wild Goose Chase" (page 61); and instructions for the Liberated Squares-on-Point border are found in "Process 7: Liberated Square-Within-a-Square" (page 90).

SCRAPPY MEDALLION (page 104) was definitely the result of using what I had on hand, including both reproduction and contemporary fabrics. In fact, if you look carefully, you'll see that the corner squares and some other parts of the quilt are cut from the same fabric line I used to make LORRAINE'S MEDALLION (page 101).

This is a good example of a quilt that pretty much designed itself because it was made from little scraps that had to be joined in the most practical way possible to be of use. The result is a quilt more imaginative in design than most of us could come up with by preplanning it.

The entire center panel (inside the purple frame) was pieced from scraps I literally picked up off the floor at my 2002 Beaver Island Quilt Retreat. I wrapped string-pieced borders around the center panel until those ran out, and then finished with Square-Within-a-Square blocks pieced from leftovers. Then came some wholecloth borders punctuated with corner squares. You can understand the order in which I added the borders by following the seam lines.

SCRAPPY MEDALLION, 32" x 37", 2002. Made and machine quilted by the author. The center panel and most of the pieced work was made from "floor scraps" collected at my Beaver Island Quilt Retreat in 2002.

LEFT: SCRAPPY MEDALLION, detail. Full quilt on page 104. As I often do, in this quilt I added a strip of different fabric to make a border long enough.

I machine quilted the border of this quilt in a Liberated Sawtooth design that I did not mark beforehand. I used my usual technique of not lifting the feed dogs, which my old, reliable cast-iron Singer® doesn't do. And lastly, I made a "strong finish" with a wide single-width binding cut on the straight of the goods.

Let's begin studying BITS AND PIECES (page 106) where it began—in the middle. The center panel begins with leftover irregular squares, strips, and rectangles sewn together and framed in pink. This Liberated centerpiece is surrounded on three sides by a string-pieced border, also composed completely of leftovers, and on the remaining side with leftover half-square triangles. Notice that the half-square-triangle border ends with a partial unit. This is a time-honored method for adding borders and also a very Liberated way. It's a practical solution for piecing the border, sewing it on to the quilt, and trimming or lengthening the border when you "come to the end," in spite of where the end might fall.

This center section is framed with a wholecloth blue border and Liberated scrappy corner squares. Another wholecloth border follows, made with two different prints, a non-decision prompted by the fact that I didn't have enough of either print to go all the way around. Liberated Stars fill the corners of this border. All four Star blocks are very scrappy, with star points made from a variety of fabrics. Two blocks have pieced Liberated center squares.

Next comes a bubble-gum pink wholecloth border with blue corner squares. This calm border supplies a needed visual break in an otherwise busy quilt.

Then here comes a traditionally pieced Wild Goose Chase border, a typical choice for an early medallion quilt. If you look at each border, you'll see that it *begins* with a whole goose, while *two end* with just a partial goose. Here's the thing about that: first, it's likely you wouldn't even notice this oddity if I didn't point it out; and secondly, in no way does it negatively affect the artfulness of the quilt.

Liberated Stars repeat in the corners of the Wild Goose Chase border, while a narrow wholecloth outer border and corner squares repeat colors in previous borders.

Finally, Robyn House machine quilted the entire quilt with a series of feather designs to reinforce the traditional look.

BITS AND PIECES, 54" x 56", 2002. Made by the author and machine quilted by Robyn House.

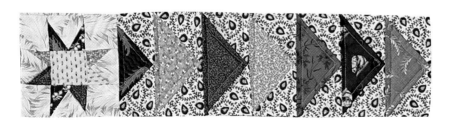

LEFT: BITS AND PIECES, detail. The idea that borders "should" come out evenly derives from the notion that the most important aspect of a quilt is the precision with which the pieces fit together—an idea that has absolutely *nothing* to do with art.

My WELSH MEDALLION was directly inspired by a quilt shown in *The Quilts of the British Isles* by Janet Rae (see Bibliography, page 125). The original quilt began with a center panel of toile de Jouy. The borders were pieced in uneven lengths of various fabrics, suggesting that it was, in fact, a scrap quilt made of leftovers that weren't resized, but used just as they were. I used these same ideas in my quilt.

BELOW: WELSH MEDALLION, 34" x 40", 2003. Made and hand quilted by the author. Inspired by a child's quilt c. 1849–1877 shown in *The Quilts of the British Isles* by Janet Rae (see Bibliography, page 125).

Welsh Medallion, detail. Full quilt on page 107. In homage to the quilt that inspired it, I began my quilt with a toile de Jouy panel, and surrounded it with borders of randomly arranged squares and strips.

With any style of quilt, it is important to measure and pin the borders with care so your finished quilt will lie flat and not waffle along the edges. Since a medallion quilt is made with multiple borders, good border technique will come in especially handy.

Step-by-Step: Liberated Medallion

I have made quite a few medallion quilts and always feel like it is one of the best ways to design a quilt. You don't have to figure out anything further than the next border. In viewing antique medallions, I've discovered wholecloth borders are common, and that pieced borders are generally simple, made up of Squares on Point, any and all Sawtooth variations, Wild Geese, Broken Dishes, and Pinwheels blocks.

1. Start by choosing (or designing) a square or rectangular center panel around which everything else will revolve.

2. Beginning with the innermost border, decide what kind of border you want to add (wholecloth or pieced) and how wide you want it to be. Work just one border at a time. Make some borders using your favorite Liberated blocks or techniques, sew the borders to the center panel, and don't worry about what happens if a border fits or not. Just sew it on, and cut off the extra or add more as needed.

3. Press each border as you finish it. Measure the border to fit the quilt and trim the border to that size. I suggest that you pay no attention to making the borders work out perfectly at the ends. This Liberated approach to corners is one of the great solutions figured out by our ancestors long ago. If you look at the ends of the rows or the corner turns on antique medallion quilts, you'll very often see evidence of this casual treatment, which continues to work wonderfully well today.

4. Quilt and hang the finished quilt on your wall or place it on you bed for your friends to admire.

PROCESS 9: Liberated Samplers

I have always loved old-fashioned sampler quilts that were put together with orphan (odd or leftover) blocks in ways that were obviously chosen because they were practical. I continue to love seeing how artistic, how full of unexpected surprises these quilts can be, and how cleverly they defy the predictable.

In the world of Liberated Quiltmaking—where I spend a considerable amount of time—I have found that I collect and save a fair number of orphan blocks. My ultimate goal is to place them in a good home. This works out easily, because they seem to live together happily: Log Cabins obviously coexist happily with Houses, but Shoo Fly, Churn Dash, and Star blocks get along fine, too.

I've also made Liberated Samplers with new, rather than leftover blocks. I begin by choosing a style of fabrics—for example, historical reproduction prints, 1930s reproduction prints, or contemporary prints—and use them to make a variety of blocks that are all the same size. SISTERS SAMPLER (page 111) and SAMPLER WITH LOG CABINS, STARS, AND HOUSES (page 112) are examples.

At other times, I make some Liberated blocks in *relatively* the same scale, but with no predetermined measurements that would ensure that the blocks will fit together. You can see this approach in SAMPLER (page 114).

RIGHT: SISTERS SAMPLER, detail. Full quilt on page 111.

Sampler with Log Cabins, Stars, and Houses, detail. Full quilt on page 112. Sometimes I make all my sampler blocks in the same size, which makes them very easy to fit together.

Let's Look at the Quilts

Let's take a closer look at these Liberated Sampler quilts to see what they are made of.

Sisters Sampler (page 111) is made with fabrics designed by Valori Wells of The Stitchin' Post (Sisters, OR) fame. Not often do I make a quilt with a single line of fabric, but these fabrics drew me in and I couldn't resist. The delightful zinnia prints suggested the border treatment, and also sparked the idea of using them as plain blocks to mix with their pieced "sisters."

The fact that the blocks aren't arranged in any particular way adds to the visual interest of this quilt. Liberated Stars, Gwenny's Pinwheels, and plain blocks show up randomly from row to row.

Sampler, detail. Full quilt on page 114. Sometimes I make the blocks "sort of" the same size. Putting the quilt together is like assembling a jigsaw puzzle, with you adding the necessary bits and pieces to make it fit.

Sisters Sampler, detail. Full quilt on page 111. The zinnia prints made a natural, effective—and easy—border treatment for this "flower-ful" quilt.

SISTERS SAMPLER, 57" x 72", 2006. Made by the author and machine quilted by Robyn House.

In SAMPLER WITH LOG CABINS, STARS, AND HOUSES, Liberated Log Cabins, Houses, Stars, and one Shoo Fly block join together in a playful way. In this quilt, I squared all the blocks to the same size, and pieced the inside border with four different black prints. The outer border print saved me lots of work: It looks pieced, but it's not! I tied this quilt on the front with multicolored floss, adding to the casual look.

BELOW: SAMPLER WITH LOG CABINS, STARS, AND HOUSES, 44" x 50", 1999. Made and tied with multicolored floss by the author.

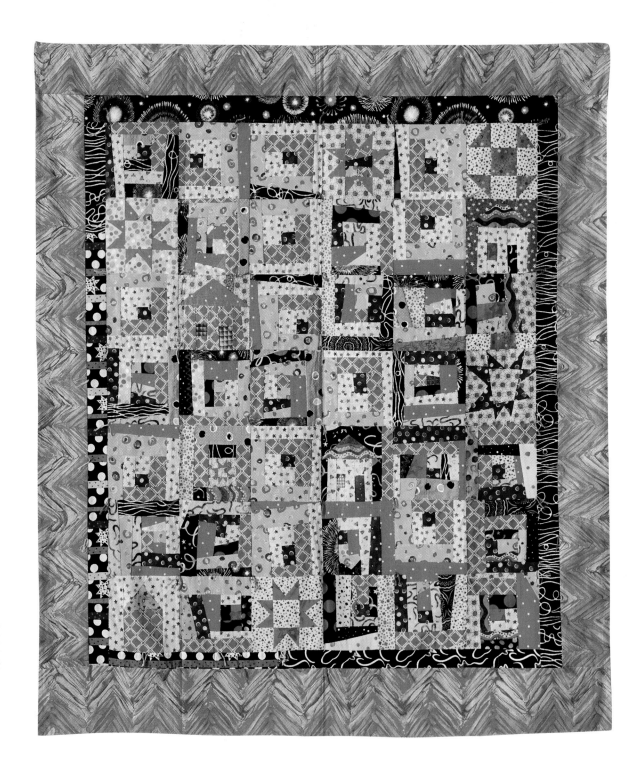

SAMPLER WITH STRING BLOCKS AND APPLIQUÉ BORDER is a quilt built on ideas that are timeless. Here we have Liberated Stars mixed with leftover Churn Dashes, a random Shoo Fly block, and a block made with half-square triangles, all tossed with string-pieced blocks turning this way and that. The design continues its old-fashioned ways with a Liberated Vine border, which I placed by eye, ignoring the concept of corner resolution. It finishes with a classic Sawtooth border and overall fan quilting.

BELOW: SAMPLER WITH STRING BLOCKS AND APPLIQUÉ BORDER, 44" x 50", 2006. Made by the author and machine quilted by Robyn House.

Sᴀᴍᴘʟᴇʀ, 29" x 25", 2002. Made by the author and machine quilted by
Robyn House.

As I was writing this chapter, it occurred to me to suggest that
you work your way through the book, making samples of all the
ideas presented, and then put these samples into a memory quilt of
your trip through these pages. My next thought was, "Well Gwen,
why don't you do that?" and thus my Lɪʙᴇʀᴀᴛᴇᴅ Sᴀᴍᴘʟᴇʀ (page
115). This quilt is a collection of blocks from this book, plus a few
orphan Liberated blocks I had on hand. What a charming quilt this
would be for a baby!

ABOVE: LIBERATED SAMPLER, 34" x 38", 2009. Made by the author and machine quilted by Robyn House.

LEFT: LIBERATED SAMPLER, details. This little blue Basket block and these two tiny Four Patch blocks are conventionally pieced and just managed to sneak into my quilt when no one was looking.

I LOVE PURPLE was made by Karen Setla, who knows what she's doing in the quilt department. In my circle, she also has a well-deserved reputation for her close, all-over hand quilting. Karen makes good-sized quilts, and quilts many of them in fans with the lines of quilting only ½" apart. See her LIBERATED BASKET (page 54) in "Process 4: Liberated Baskets" and her LIBERATED SHOO FLY (page 35) in "Process 2: Base-Block Construction" for two more examples.

I LOVE PURPLE, detail. Check out the amazing all-over hand quilting that enhances Karen Setla's Liberated Sampler.

I LOVE PURPLE, 70" x 96", 2004. Made and hand quilted by Karen Setla, Bath, MI.

GALLERY: Great Quilts by Liberated Quilters

Over the years, I have been delighted to see many very fine quilts as I've traveled around the country. I so often see work that does not get shown broadly, but is just extraordinarily fine. Here are some exciting quilts made by quilters who understand the concepts of Liberated Quiltmaking and who have taken the concept in new and exciting directions. That they have confidence in technical skills enables them to concentrate on the artistic aspects of their work. It's such a pleasure for me to be able to show these notable quilts made by notable men and women in this book.

CUPLETS, 50" x 50", 2009. Made by Joyce Hart, Delta, IA, and quilted by Cindy Atwood.

Joyce applied free-piecing techniques to create a variety of colorful coffee cups in different shapes and sizes. In true Liberated fashion, she assembled the quilt jigsaw-puzzle style, filling in the gaps with a wide assortment of pieced and plain filler strips.

BERRY THICKET, 80" x 80", 2006. Made and quilted By Pat Probst, Columbus, IN.

Pat is an accomplished woman—serious gardener, great cook, talented rug hooker—and excellent quiltmaker, both technically and artistically. I've seen many of her quilts over the years and have always admired the fact that her work is both well constructed and artistically profound—evidence that having good technique enables you to successfully accomplish what you envision. In BERRY THICKET, notice—among other great Liberated elements—the original, hand appliquéd Liberated twiggy border!

EXPERIMENT IN ABSTRACT, 31¼" x 43½", 2009. Made by Cathy Jones, Beaver Island, MI, and machine quilted by Rogene Fischer.

Cathy has been quilting for over 30 years, and—with this quilt—she "ventured out of her comfort zone, not only in color, but in design" to create her first abstract quilt. At one point, she thought she had finished it, but something still seemed missing, so she added the red circle. Is it any wonder that she "absolutely loves" the finished product?

FREE RANGE: LIBERATED CHICKENS, 30" x 35", 1998. Made and quilted by
Kristin Otte, Goleta, CA.

Kristin tried her hand at Liberated Stars, but noticed they looked a lot more
like chickens…so she went with it.

Two Sisters, 41½" x 55", 2002. Made and hand quilted with #8 perle cotton by Allyn Adell Humphrey, Arlington, VA.

Allyn is another quilter whom I've known for quite a few years, and whose work demonstrates a very clear artistic voice. She hand quilts most of her work using a big stitch and often quilts very close all-over fans for a great effect.

Table Scraps: #126 – 176/1429, 36" x 57", 2000. Made and machine quilted by Kathy Peters, Marquette, MI.

Kathy began making Liberated Chair blocks and has made quite a few
wonderful chair quilts. The quilt shown here was made from a scrap bag of
fabric from the 1970s given to her by a neighbor.

LEFT: THERE GOES THE NEIGHBOR-HOOD, 19" x 17", 2003. Made, hand quilted, and embellished by Joshua Durst, Heiskell, TN.

Joshua refers to this quilt as his (blush, blush) "Ode to Gwen." It was created for a challenge issued by the Smoky Mountain Quilters Guild of Tennessee. The entire quilt, including the tiny quilt in the upper-right block, was pieced using Liberated Quiltmaking techniques. The surface is heavily hand quilted and embellished with buttons, beads, and other goodies.

RIGHT: ALPHABET SAMPLER, 36" x 38", 2000. Made and quilted by Tonya Ricucci, Palm Beach Gardens, FL.

Tonya loves making Liberated quilts. She figured out how to make Liberated letters and has been sharing her ideas on her blog for quite a few years now.

RED OWLS, 38" x 52", 2007. Made and hand quilted by Karin Pierce, Belmont, ME.

Liberated quilts also come in appliqué form as you can see by the RED OWLS. This dazzling creation was made by Karin Pierce, who I see as a natural-born Liberated quilter. Her work is often astonishing and startling in its directness, boldness, and originality. When I see her work, I feel as though I should get up and go sit in the back row. Great work!

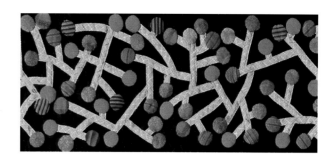

BIBLIOGRAPHY

Books About African-American Quilts and Quilters

Arnett, William. *Gee's Bend: The Women and Their Quilts*. Atlanta, Georgia: Tinwood Books, 2002.

Arnett, William, Alvia Wardlaw, Jane Livingston, and John Beardsley. *Quilts of Gee's Bend: Masterpieces from a Lost Place*. Atlanta, Georgia: Tinwood Books, 2002.

Benberry, Cuesta. *Always There: The African-American Presence in American Quilts*. Louisville, Kentucky: The Kentucky Quilt Project, Inc., 1992.

Cubbs, Joanne, Dana Friis-Hansen, and Matt Arnett. *Mary Lee Bendolph. Gee's Bend Quilts, and Beyond*. Atlanta, Georgia: Tinwood Books, 2006.

Fry, Gladys-Marie. *Stitched from the Soul: Slave Quilts from the Ante-Bellum South*. New York: Dutton Studio Books with the Museum of American Folk Art, 1990.

Grudin, Eva Ungar. *Stitching Memories: African-American Story Quilts*. Williamstown, Massachusetts: Williams College Museum of Art, 1990.

Heffley, Scott. *Bold Improvisation: Searching for African-American Quilts*. Kansas City, Missouri: Kansas City Star Books, 2007.

Leon, Eli. *Accidentally on Purpose: The Aesthetic Management of Irregularities in African Textiles and African-American Quilts*. Davenport, Iowa: Figge Art Museum, 2006.

..........*Something Pertaining to God: The Patchwork Art of Rosie Lee Tompkins*. Burlington, Vermont: Shelburne Museum, 2007.

.... *Who'd A Thought It: Improvisation in Afririan-American Quiltmaking*. San Francisco, California: San Francisco Craft and Folk Art Museum, 1988.

Vlach, John Michael. *The Afro-American Tradition in Decorative Arts*. Cleveland, Ohio: The Cleveland Museum of Art, 1978.

Wahlam, Maude Southwell. *Signs and Symbols: African Images in African-American Quilts*. New York: Studio Books in Association with the Museum of American Folk Art. 1993.

Watts, Katherine and Elizabeth Walker. *Anna Williams: Her Quilts and Their Influences*. Paducah, Kentucky: American Quilter's Society, 1995.

Books Showing Gwen's Liberated Quilts

Marston, Gwen. *Ideas and Inspirations: Abstract Quilts in Solids*. Gwen Marston/San Jose, California: MoCa Press, 2008.

..........*Liberated Quiltmaking*. Paducah, Kentucky: American Quilter's Society, 1996.

..........*Liberated String Quilts*. Lafayette, California: C&T Publishing, 2003

Moran, Freddy and Gwen Marston. *Collaborative Quilting*. New York: Sterling Publishing Co, Inc., 2006.

............*Freddy and Gwen Collaborate Again*. New York: Sterling Publishing Co, Inc., 2009.

Additional References

Quilts of Virginia, 1607–1899: The Birth of America Through The Eye of A Needle. Atglen, Pennsylvania: Schiffer Publishing, 2006.

Rae, Janet. *The Quilts of the British Isles*. New York: Plume, 1987.

INDEX of Quilts

ABOUT the Author

Gwen Marston is a professional quiltmaker, author, and teacher. She has taught quilting nationally and internationally for over three decades. Her articles have appeared in many magazines throughout the years. This is her twenty-fourth book.

Gwen's work has been shown in many group exhibits throughout the United States and abroad, and also in 21 solo exhibits, including seven solo exhibits of her small quilts. Collaborative quilts made by Gwen and Freddy Moran have been shown at The National Quilt Museum in Paducah, Kentucky, and in four other exhibits.

For 27 years, Gwen has offered a series of quilting retreats in the fall for serious students of quiltmaking.

Gwen lives and works at her home on Beaver Island, Michigan.

Previously Published Books by Gwen

70 Classic Quilting Patterns (with Joe Cunningham). Dover Publications, Inc., 1987.

American Beauties: Rose and Tulip Quilts (with Joe Cunningham). AQS, 1988.

Amish Quilting Patterns (with Joe Cunningham). Dover Publications, Inc., 1987.

Classic Four-Block Appliqué Quilts: A Back-to-Basics Approach. C&T Publishing, 2005.

Collaborative Quilting (with Freddy Moran). Sterling Publishing, Inc., 2006.

Fabric Picture Books. AQS, 2002.

Freddy & Gwen Collaborate Again (with Freddy Moran). Sterling Publishing, Inc., 2006.

Gwen Marston's Quilting & Appliqué Patterns. AQS, 2006.

Ideas and Inspirations: Abstract Quilts in Solids. MoCa Press, 2008.

Liberated Quiltmaking. AQS, 1996.

Liberated String Quilts. C&T Publishing, 2003.

Lively Little Folk-Art Quilts. C&T Publishing, 2003.

Mary Schafer and Her Quilts (with Joe Cunningham). Michigan State University Press, 1990.

Mary Schafer, American Quilt Maker. The University of Michigan Press, 2004. Winner of the Michigan Notable Book Award for Literature in 2005.

Q Is For Quilt. Michigan State University Press, 1987.

Quilting with Style: Principles for Great Pattern Design (with Joe Cunningham). AQS, 1993.

Sets and Borders (with Joe Cunningham). AQS, 1987.

Twenty Little Amish Quilts. Dover Publications, Inc., 1993.

Twenty Little Four Patch Quilts. Dover Publications, Inc., 1996.

Twenty Little Log Cabin Quilts. Dover Publications, Inc., 1995.

Twenty Little Patchwork Quilts (with Joe Cunningham). Dover Publications, Inc., 1990.

Twenty Little Pinwheel Quilts. Dover Publications, Inc., 1994.

Twenty Little Triangle Quilts. Dover Publications, Inc., 1997.

For today's quilter...
inspiration and creativity from

AQS Publishing

Weekend QUILTS
Judy Laquidara

Kimberly Einmo
JELLY ROLL QUILTS & MORE

BLOCK *Beauty* QUILTS
AQS Publishing
Donna Poster

AQS Publishing
SQUARE MAGIC
QUILTS
Michelle J. Linder

Rule-Breaking Quilts
Kathryn SCHMIDT
AQS Publishing

AQS Publishing
Patchwork 4 Ways
Kathleen Hulett

LOOK for these books nationally.
CALL or **VISIT** our Web site:

1-800-626-5420
www.AmericanQuilter.com